A Vegan Taste of East Africa

Also by Linda Majzlik

A VEGAN TASTE OF EAST AFRICA

Linda Majzlik

JON CARPENTER

Our books may be ordered from bookshops or (post free) from
Jon Carpenter Publishing, Alder House, Market Street, Charlbury,
England OX7 3PH

Credit card orders may be phoned or faxed to 01689 870437
or 01608 811969

First published in 2005 by
Jon Carpenter Publishing
Alder House, Market Street, Charlbury, Oxfordshire OX7 3PH
☎ 01608 811969

Reprinted 2007, 2010

© Linda Majzlik 2005

ISBN 978-1-897766-97-2

Printed in England by CPI Antony Rowe, Chippenham

CONTENTS

Main courses

Breads

Salads

Cakes and pastries

Drinks

INTRODUCTION

The Sudan, Ethiopia, Eritrea, Djibouti, the Somali Republic, Kenya, Uganda, Rwanda, Burundi and Tanzania make up the region known as East Africa, a huge and geographically extreme part of the continent. Within this region the diverse terrain varies from vast areas of inhospitable desert, densely forested highlands, semi-arid lowlands, huge expanses of savanna and high snow-capped mountain ranges, to great lakes and swampy areas and miles of tropical sandy beaches. Although much of the land is unsuitable for cultivating crops, there are pockets of very favourable growing conditions. In these areas a wide variety of crops is grown, including various grains, sugar cane, nuts, tea, coffee, spices and an abundance of vegetables and tropical fruits.

However, farming in many rural areas is a hazardous business, with farmers having to contend with little rainfall or drought, soil erosion and even the occasional plague of locusts which can devastate fields of crops in minutes. Some of the principal food crops that are widely grown, therefore, have proved over time to be relatively resistant to these natural hazards. Examples include millet, teff and sorghum, all staple grains which are able to grow in poor soils with little rainfall; peanuts, which thrive in semi-arid conditions; and cassava, a root crop which can be grown in shifting systems and is resistant to locust attacks and drought. This starchy staple is also resistant to spoilage underground and can be harvested as and when needed, a great stand-by for when other food is scarce. Use is also made of the lowland swampy areas, where rice is widely cultivated.

Many of the staple foods that are now associated with East Africa were in fact brought there by various early explorers and settlers. Beans, cassavas, sweet potatoes, peanuts and maize were all originally from America and were taken to Africa by European explorers. Citrus fruits, chillies, peppers, tomatoes and pineapples were reportedly introduced by Portuguese settlers as long ago as the late 15th century, while plantains are believed to have come from Asia. Cinnamon, cloves and nutmeg, three important spices grown on large plantations on the exotic islands of Zanzibar and Pemba, were brought in from the Molucca Islands in Indonesia. As well as being a major export, they are used all over the region to flavour a variety of sweet and savoury dishes. The popularity of curry dishes in some areas is a legacy of the Indians who were invited to Uganda by the British to help construct the railways. More recently parts of Ethiopia were occupied by Italy and Italian food has since been incorporated into the traditional cuisine, especially in Eritrea, where pizza and pasta dishes are great favourites.

East Africa is a region of contrasts and home to literally hundreds of ethnic and tribal groups, who speak a variety of languages and have many different religions. One aspect that many of these groups have in common, however, is the kind of meals eaten, which for most people are based around a starchy staple such as a grain or root vegetable dish, accompanied by thick, flavourful soups and stews and speciality breads.

The starchy part of the meal is commonly rolled into a hollowed ball with the fingers of the right hand and then used to scoop up other foods. Because cutlery is rare it is important for the hands to be cleansed before the meal begins and in many countries hand washing both before and after meals is a ritual. Before the meal starts a jug and bowl are brought in and water is poured over the diners' hands, which are held over the bowl. A towel is passed around to dry the hands and the same thing is done again at the end of the meal.

Entertaining guests is seen as a great honour in many East African households and extra food is often prepared just in case any unexpected diners arrive. Recipes are not generally written down, but are passed on by word of mouth or simply created by the cook by experimenting with what ingredients are available.

East African cuisine is sadly often overlooked outside the region, with many people believing that it consists only of starchy tasteless stodge! Hopefully this book will help dispel that myth and show that instead there are dozens of creative, richly-flavoured traditional dishes made from an exciting array of exotic and nutritious ingredients. As all the basic ingredients are plant-based the recipes are eminently suitable for vegans and with many of the dishes extremely quick and easy to prepare they should also appeal to vegans who have little time to cook.

THE VEGAN EAST AFRICAN STORECUPBOARD

Many of the essential staples of the region such as cassavas, maize, plantains, potatoes, squashes, sweet potatoes and yams have a long shelf-life if stored in a cool dark place and these are combined with a sometimes limited selection of storecupboard ingredients to provide an array of imaginative and satisfying sweet and savoury dishes.

Almonds Rich in protein, vitamins and calcium, almonds are a popular ingredient in Somalia, where they are combined with potatoes to make a traditional soup.

Barley A staple crop in Ethiopia, barley is served plainly cooked or mixed with vegetables as an accompaniment for stews. Pot barley is more nutritious than pearl, which has been stripped of many nutrients in the milling process.

Beans Although tinned beans are a useful standby, it is worth cooking dried beans in bulk and freezing them. All beans provide protein, fibre and minerals and varieties that are especially popular in East Africa are blackeye and red kidney.

Cashew nuts A good source of protein and minerals. Widely grown in Tanzania where they are an important export crop, cashew nuts are enjoyed in sweet and savoury dishes and their flavour is enhanced by lightly toasting.

Chickpeas These creamy, nutty-flavoured peas combine well with all other ingredients and are commonly used in all kinds of savoury dishes. They are highly nutritious and rich in protein, fibre, vitamins and minerals.

Chillies Widely grown in Kenya and exported to many other countries, fresh chillies are an essential ingredient all over the region. They keep well in the refrigerator for up to 10 days.

Coconut Not a true nut but the fruit of the coconut palm, which grows abundantly along the coastal areas of East Africa. Used in its various forms, coconut adds richness and flavour to sweet and savoury dishes.

Creamed This is pure fresh coconut flesh shaped into a vacuum-packed block. Once opened the block needs to be kept in the fridge and used within a couple of weeks. For longer storage, grate the block and freeze it.

Desiccated The dried flesh of the coconut is often used for sprinkling over cakes and flans before baking.

Flaked Flakes of dried coconut flesh are used to garnish both sweet and savoury dishes. Lightly toasting the flakes enhances the flavour.

Milk A rich thick liquid made from pressed coconut flesh, this is available tinned or in cartons. Thinned and low-fat versions are also available. Coconut milk can also be made by dissolving 4oz/100g grated creamed coconut in 20 fl.oz/600ml hot water, or by blending 6oz/175g desiccated coconut with 20 fl.oz/600ml hot water and straining it though a fine sieve or muslin bag, pressing out as much liquid as possible. Any unused coconut milk can be frozen.

Cornflour A very fine starchy white flour milled from corn. It is sometimes known as cornstarch and is used for thickening.

Cornmeal Ground yellow maize, also known as maizemeal. Cornmeal can be bought in many grades from fine to coarse, but in many parts of East Africa dried corncobs are ground by hand in a mortar. The resulting meal is used in particular for making ugali and cornbread.

Groundnut oil An essential cooking oil made from peanuts. It is used extensively for frying, for making dressings and as an ingredient in bread and cake recipes. The oil is bland-tasting and can be heated to high temperatures without burning.

Herbs Fresh herbs are preferred and these are home-grown or bought together with fresh vegetables in the market.

Coriander A uniquely flavoured herb and the most widely used in all kinds of savoury dishes across the region.

Parsley A universally popular herb, parsley is used as an ingredient in many savoury dishes or chopped and sprinkled on cooked dishes as a garnish.

Lemon juice Portuguese settlers introduced citrus fruits to the continent and lemon juice is widely used as a flavouring in various savoury dishes.

Lentils A staple food, commonly used across the region to make soups, stews and salads, or simply served plainly cooked. All lentils are highly nutritious and a rich source of protein, fibre, vitamins and minerals.

Millet A drought-resistant crop which thrives in hot climates and nutrient-deficient soils where other crops fail to grow. Millet is an important staple food all over East Africa and is served plainly cooked or mixed with vegetables. The grain has a mild, delicate, nutty flavour and is rich in protein and iron.

Millet flour A distinctively-flavoured greyish-coloured flour which is used extensively to make various types of bread. In areas where millet is more widely available than maize, millet flour is used instead of cornmeal to make ugali.

Peanuts Brought to Africa by Spanish explorers, peanuts, or groundnuts as they are called in East Africa, are widely grown and are an important cash-crop for farmers. They grow well in semi-arid conditions and are used extensively in sweet and savoury recipes. The nuts are traditionally ground by pounding them in a mortar with a pestle, and then roasted to enrich their flavour. An excellent source of protein, minerals and vitamins.

Peanut butter Known as groundnut paste in East Africa, smooth and crunchy versions are used in sweet and savoury dishes.

Rice A staple crop in the Sudan and in Tanzania, where it is mainly grown in wetter lowland areas. Large quantities of cooked rice are served as an accompaniment for stews and curries. It is also used with other savoury ingredients in biriani-style dishes or mixed with sweet ingredients and served as a pudding.

Rice flour A gluten-free flour milled from rice, it is often combined with wheat flour to make various breads and cakes.

Root ginger An essential ingredient in numerous savoury dishes, fresh root ginger adds 'heat' and a spicy, fragrant flavour. To store fresh root ginger, cut it into useable portions and freeze.

Soya milk Unsweetened soya milk has been used in recipes requiring milk.

Spices East African cooks prefer to use whole dried spices and grind them in a mortar when required.

Allspice Tasting of a mixture of cinnamon, cloves and nutmeg, allspice is a favourite flavouring for various sweet dishes.

Berbere A hot Ethiopian spice blend which is not widely available ready-made, but can easily be made at home.

>   8 small dried red chillies
>
>   8 cardamom pods, husked
>
>   1 rounded teaspoon paprika
>
>   1 teaspoon cumin seeds
>
>   1 teaspoon fenugreek seeds
>
>   1 teaspoon coriander seeds
>
>   1 teaspoon ground ginger
>
>   1 teaspoon black peppercorns
>
>   ½ teaspoon allspice berries
>
>   ¼ teaspoon turmeric
>
>   ¼ teaspoon ground cinnamon
>
>   6 cloves

Put the chillies, cardamom, cumin, fenugreek and coriander seeds, peppercorns, allspice and cloves in a small pan and heat gently until an aroma is given off, stirring constantly to prevent burning. Remove from the heat and grind the spices to a powder. Add the paprika, ground ginger, turmeric and cinnamon and mix thoroughly.

Black pepper A universally popular seasoning for savoury dishes, black peppercorns are ground by hand in a mortar.

Cardamom This pine-fragranced spice is available in three forms – as pods, seeds or ground. The pods vary in colour but it is generally agreed that the green variety is the most flavourful and aromatic. Seeds are used whole or ground in various sweet and savoury dishes.

Cayenne pepper The dried fruit of a hot red pepper, deep red in colour and very pungent. Cayenne is used to add 'heat' to a dish.

Chilli Chilli powder is occasionally used to add 'heat' to savoury dishes.

Cinnamon Used both as sticks and ground, cinnamon has a warm, comforting, sweet flavour and is a popular ingredient in sweet and savoury recipes

Cloves The dried buds of an evergreen tree which are valued for their anaesthetic and antiseptic properties. Whole cloves are used to flavour savoury rice dishes and ground cloves are a favourite flavouring in sweet recipes.

Coriander The dried seed of a plant which belongs to the parsley family. Coriander seeds have a mild, sweet, orangey flavour which is enhanced when the seeds are crushed.

Cumin Used both as whole seeds and ground, cumin has a strong earthy flavour and is regularly used in all kinds of savoury dishes.

Curry powder East African cooks prefer to make their own special blends of curry powder by grinding their own traditional combinations of dried whole spices. Unfortunately these are rarely written down, so ready-made medium-hot blends have been used in the recipes here.

Fenugreek Valued for its ability to soothe the intestines, fenugreek has a bitter-sweet flavour and is always used sparingly.

Ginger The ground dried root has a strong spicy but sweet flavour and adds a more mellow gingery taste than the fresh variety.

Paprika Made by grinding dried sweet red peppers, paprika is used to add colour and a mild sweet flavour to savoury dishes, especially those containing tomatoes.

Turmeric A bright-yellow spice which is the powdered rhizome of a plant belonging to the ginger family. It is valued for its anti-bacterial properties and adds colour and a distinctive earthy pungency to various savoury dishes.

Split peas A rich source of protein, fibre, minerals and vitamins, split peas are a favourite ingredient in Ethiopia for making thick nutritious soups.

Tamarind The fruit of a large tropical tree, tamarind is used to add sourness to savoury dishes and is especially popular in Swahili cookery. It is usually sold in sticky blocks consisting of crushed pods, which need to be soaked in hot water to produce a purée. Jars of ready-made purée are also available.

Textured vegetable protein A nutritious and versatile soya product, which readily absorbs the flavours of other ingredients. The natural minced variety is used here in a few savoury recipes.

Tomato purée Used to strengthen the flavour of and add colour to tomato-based dishes.

Vegetable stock Instead of making their own vegetable stock, East African cooks are more likely to use vegetable stock cubes. Always check ingredient labels, as many vegetable stock cubes contain animal-derived ingredients.

Yeast Easy-blend dried yeast is used in the recipes requiring yeast. It does not need to be reconstituted in liquid.

Yoghurt Yoghurt-based dressings and salads are especially popular accompaniments for curry dishes and plain soya yoghurt is used here.

SOUPS

A wide variety of soups is enjoyed across the region and these are all easily prepared from fresh wholesome ingredients. Thin soups, especially those made with ground nuts, are served as starters in many countries, while the thicker heartier soups are a meal in themselves when served with a starchy accompaniment and bread. Soups made from dried peas are especially popular in Ethiopia and are eaten during Lent and on fasting days when no meat may be eaten.

Sweet potato and cashew nut soup (serves 4)

1¼lb/550g sweet potatoes, peeled and diced

4oz/100g tomato, skinned and chopped

1 red onion, peeled and finely chopped

1 small red chilli, deseeded and finely chopped

2 garlic cloves, crushed

1 dessertspoon groundnut oil

½ teaspoon ground ginger

½ teaspoon paprika

black pepper

20 fl.oz/600ml vegetable stock or water

2oz/50g cashew nuts, ground and roasted

roasted chopped cashew nuts

Fry the onion, chilli and garlic in the oil until soft, then add the sweet potatoes, tomato, ginger, paprika and stock and season with black pepper. Stir well and bring to the boil, cover and simmer for about 10 minutes until the potatoes are tender. Stir in the ground cashews and continue simmering for 2 minutes, then ladle the soup into serving bowls and sprinkle with chopped cashews.

Ethiopian dried pea soup (serves 4)

8oz/225g split green peas

1 large red onion, peeled and chopped

4 garlic cloves, crushed

1 green chilli, deseeded and finely chopped

1 tablespoon groundnut oil

1 teaspoon ground ginger

black pepper

finely chopped fresh coriander

Soak the split peas in water overnight. Drain and rinse and put in a pan with fresh water. Bring to the boil, cover and simmer briskly for 30 minutes. Drain over a bowl and keep the cooking liquid.

Fry the onion in the oil in a large pan for 10 minutes. Add the peas, garlic, chilli and ginger and season with black pepper. Make the cooking liquid up to 30 fl.oz/900ml with water and add to the pan, stir well and bring to the boil. Cover and simmer, stirring occasionally, for about 40 minutes until the peas are done and the soup is thick. Serve garnished with chopped coriander.

Okra and blackeye bean soup (serves 4)

8oz/225g okra, topped, tailed and cut into ½ inch/1cm diagonal slices

8oz/225g cooked blackeye beans

8oz/225g tomatoes, skinned and chopped

1 red onion, peeled and finely chopped

1 green chilli, deseeded and finely chopped

2 garlic cloves, crushed

20 fl.oz/600ml vegetable stock or water

1 dessertspoon groundnut oil

2 tablespoons tomato purée

2 teaspoons ground cumin

1 teaspoon paprika

black pepper

Fry the onion, chilli and garlic in the oil until softened. Add the tomatoes and spices and cook for a couple of minutes until pulpy. Now add the remaining ingredients and stir well. Bring to the boil, cover and simmer for about 15 minutes until cooked.

Courgette, cauliflower and coconut soup (serves 4)

8oz/225g courgettes, chopped

8oz/225g cauliflower, cut into tiny florets

6oz/175g tomatoes, skinned and chopped

1 red onion, peeled and finely chopped

1 garlic clove, crushed

1 small red chilli, deseeded and finely chopped

1 dessertspoon groundnut oil

2 tablespoons finely chopped fresh coriander

1 tablespoon lemon juice

1 dessertspoon tamarind purée

1 teaspoon cumin seed

½ teaspoon ground ginger

½ teaspoon turmeric

black pepper

16 fl.oz/475ml vegetable stock or water

1oz/25g creamed coconut, grated

Soften the onion, garlic and chilli in the oil in a large pan. Add the spices, tomatoes, lemon juice and tamarind purée and stir around until pulpy, then stir in the stock, courgettes, cauliflower and coriander and bring to the boil. Cover and simmer for about 20 minutes until tender. Add the creamed coconut and stir until it dissolves before serving.

Somalian potato and almond soup (serves 4)

1¼lb/550g potatoes, peeled and diced

2oz/50g ground almonds, roasted

1 onion, peeled and finely chopped

1 dessertspoon groundnut oil

black pepper

24 fl.oz/725ml vegetable stock or water

roasted flaked almonds

In a large pan fry the onion in the oil until soft. Add the potatoes and stock and season with black pepper, then bring to the boil, cover and simmer for 15 minutes. Stir in the ground almonds and continue simmering for a couple of minutes more until the potato is done. Ladle the soup into serving bowls and sprinkle with flaked almonds.

Mixed squash and awaze soup (serves 4)

1lb/450g prepared mixed squashes (e.g. courgette, pumpkin, butternut squash), diced

1 red onion, peeled and finely chopped

1 tablespoon groundnut oil

10 fl.oz/300ml vegetable stock or water

1 quantity of awaze (see page 86)

Fry the squashes and onion in the oil for 5 minutes, stirring frequently, then pour in the stock and bring to the boil. Cover and simmer for 10 minutes, stirring occasionally. Add the awaze and mix thoroughly, then continue simmering for a few minutes until the vegetables are tender.

Peanut, carrot and corn soup (serves 4)

4oz/100g ground peanuts, roasted

8oz/225g carrots, scraped and finely chopped

8oz/225g sweetcorn kernels

1 onion, peeled and finely chopped

1 green chilli, deseeded and finely chopped

24 fl.oz/725ml water

1 dessertspoon groundnut oil

½ teaspoon ground ginger

1 rounded teaspoon ground cumin

black pepper

roasted chopped peanuts

Fry the onion and chilli in the oil until soft, then add the ginger and cumin and stir around for a few seconds. Add the carrots, sweetcorn and water, bring to the boil, cover and simmer for about 5 minutes until the carrot is cooked. Stir in the ground peanuts and season with black pepper. Bring back to the boil and simmer, stirring frequently, for about 5 minutes until the soup is thick. Ladle into serving bowls and garnish with chopped peanuts.

Yam and plantain soup (serves 4)

12oz/350g yam, peeled and finely diced

8oz/225g plantains, peeled and chopped

4oz/100g tomato, skinned and chopped

1 onion, peeled and finely chopped

1 garlic clove, crushed

1 dessertspoon groundnut oil

1 dessertspoon tamarind purée

1 teaspoon cumin seeds

22 fl.oz/650ml vegetable stock or water

black pepper

½oz/15g creamed coconut, grated

Heat the oil in a large pan and fry the onion and garlic until softened. Add the remaining ingredients except the coconut and stir well. Bring to the boil, cover and simmer, stirring frequently, for 15-20 minutes until the vegetables are done and the soup is thick. Add the coconut and stir to dissolve before serving.

Cold avocado and tomato soup (serves 4)

2 small avocados

1lb/450g tomatoes, skinned and chopped

1 red onion, peeled and finely chopped

2 garlic cloves, crushed

1 dessertspoon groundnut oil

1 tablespoon tamarind purée

2 tablespoons lemon juice

12 fl.oz/350ml water

black pepper

finely chopped fresh parsley

Soften the onion and garlic in the oil, then add the tomatoes and water, bring to the boil, cover and simmer for 3 minutes. Pass the soup through a sieve, press out as much liquid as possible with the back of a spoon and put it in the fridge until cold. Mash the avocados with the lemon juice until smooth and add to the soup together with the tamarind purée. Season with black pepper and mix well. Serve sprinkled with chopped parsley.

Spiced sweet potato soup (serves 4)

1lb/450g sweet potatoes, peeled and diced

4oz/100g tomato, skinned and chopped

1 red onion, peeled and finely chopped

1 small red chilli, deseeded and finely chopped

1 garlic clove, crushed

1 inch/2.5cm piece of root ginger, finely chopped

1 dessertspoon groundnut oil

1 rounded teaspoon ground coriander

1 rounded teaspoon ground cumin

2 cardamom pods, husked and the seeds ground

1 inch/2.5cm stick of cinnamon

¼ teaspoon turmeric

black pepper

20 fl.oz/600ml vegetable stock or water

Fry the onion and ginger in the oil until softened. Add the spices, chilli, garlic and tomato and stir around for 1 minute, then put in the sweet potatoes and stock and bring to the boil. Cover and simmer for about 15 minutes until the potato is done. Take the pan off the heat and remove the cinnamon stick. Mash the soup to break up the potato, then return to the heat and simmer for a couple of minutes, stirring constantly, until thickened.

Tanzanian mixed vegetable soup (serves 4)

6oz/175g potato, peeled and diced

6oz/175g carrots, scraped and diced

4oz/100g red pepper, chopped

4oz/100g sweetcorn kernels

4oz/100g tomato, skinned and chopped

1 onion, peeled and finely chopped

1 small green chilli, deseeded and finely chopped

1 dessertspoon groundnut oil

1 rounded teaspoon ground cumin

½ teaspoon ground ginger

⅛ teaspoon ground cinnamon

black pepper

15 fl.oz/450ml vegetable stock or water

1 rounded tablespoon peanut butter

roasted chopped peanuts

Fry the onion and chilli in the oil in a large pan until soft. Add the tomato and spices and stir around for 1 minute. Now add the other vegetables and the stock and stir well. Bring to the boil, cover and simmer for about 20 minutes until tender. Stir in the peanut butter and continue simmering and stirring until it dissolves. Ladle the soup into bowls and garnish with chopped peanuts.

Pumpkin, lentil and coconut soup (serves 4)

1lb/450g pumpkin, peeled and diced

4oz/100g brown lentils

4oz/100g tomato, skinned and chopped

½oz/15g raisins

1 onion, peeled and finely chopped

1 garlic clove, crushed

1 dessertspoon groundnut oil

1 tablespoon tomato purée

1 teaspoon curry powder

1 teaspoon cumin seeds

black pepper

12 fl.oz/350ml vegetable stock or water

1oz/25g creamed coconut, grated

Put the lentils into a large pan of water and bring to the boil. Cover and simmer for 30 minutes, then drain and set aside.

Soften the onion and garlic in the oil, add the curry powder and cumin seeds and stir around for a few seconds. Put in the tomato and cook gently until pulpy, then add the lentils, pumpkin, raisins, tomato purée and stock. Season with black pepper and combine well. Bring to the boil, cover and simmer, stirring occasionally, for about 20 minutes until the pumpkin is tender. Add the coconut and stir for a minute or so until it dissolves before serving.

Curried cabbage and bean soup (serves 4)

8oz/225g white cabbage, finely shredded

8oz/225g tomatoes, skinned and chopped

4oz/100g mixed cooked beans

2oz/50g long grain rice

1 red onion, peeled and finely chopped

1 garlic clove, crushed

1 red chilli, deseeded and finely chopped

1 dessertspoon vegetable oil

1 rounded teaspoon curry powder

¼ teaspoon ground ginger

¼ teaspoon paprika

4 cardamom pods, husked and the seeds separated

14 fl.oz/425ml vegetable stock or water

black pepper

grated creamed coconut

Fry the onion, garlic and chilli in the oil for 5 minutes, then add the spices and tomatoes and cook until soft. Add the remaining ingredients apart from the coconut and stir well. Bring to the boil, cover and simmer, stirring occasionally, for about 15 minutes until cooked. Ladle the soup into serving bowls and sprinkle with grated creamed coconut.

Peanut and ginger soup (serves 4)

8oz/225g peanuts, ground and roasted

1oz/25g root ginger, finely chopped

2 garlic cloves, crushed

1 onion, peeled and finely chopped

1 dessertspoon groundnut oil

1 teaspoon paprika

28 fl.oz/825ml vegetable stock or water

black pepper

Fry the onion, ginger and garlic in the oil until soft. Add the peanuts, paprika and stock and season with black pepper. Stir well and bring to the boil, then simmer, stirring frequently, for 5 minutes until the soup thickens.

SNACKS

Snack foods are enjoyed at all times of the day and many of the following can be bought freshly made from vendors who set up stall in bustling market places in towns and cities across the region. Freshly roasted corncobs are especially popular and these are barbecued over hot charcoal burners. Many of the spicy little snacks are inspired by the cooking styles of eastern immigrants living in various parts of the region and sambusas are an East African version of Indian samosas. Dabo kolo, an Ethiopian speciality, is flavoured with berbere, a traditional blend of spices. Some of the snacks are ideal for serving with salads, relishes and bread as more substantial meals.

Sambusas (makes 16)

dough

8oz/225g plain flour

2oz/50g vegan margarine

½ teaspoon cayenne pepper

approx. 4 fl.oz/125ml water

groundnut oil

filling

4oz/100g shelled peas

2oz/50g tomato, skinned and chopped

1½oz/40g natural minced textured vegetable protein

1 small onion, peeled and finely chopped

1 garlic clove, crushed

1 green chilli, deseeded and finely chopped

1 inch/2.5cm piece of root ginger, finely chopped

1 dessertspoon groundnut oil

1 rounded tablespoon finely chopped fresh coriander

1 teaspoon cumin seeds

1 teaspoon paprika

black pepper

6 fl.oz/175ml water

Fry the onion and ginger in the dessertspoon of oil until soft. Add the garlic, chilli and cumin seeds and stir around for a few seconds, then add the remaining filling ingredients and combine well. Bring to the boil, cover and simmer gently, stirring occasionally, for about 15 minutes, until the liquid has been absorbed and the vegetable protein is soft. Remove from the heat and allow to cool.

Mix the cayenne pepper with the flour and rub in the margarine. Add enough water to make a soft dough, then turn this out onto a floured board and knead it. Divide the dough into 8 equal pieces and roll each one into a 6 inch/15cm circle. Cut each circle in half and put them on a flat surface. Place about one rounded dessertspoonful of filling at one end of each half circle. Dampen the edges with water and fold the pastry over to enclose the filling, pinching the edges together to join.

Shallow fry the sambusas in hot oil for a few minutes on each side until golden. Drain on kitchen paper and serve warm.

Sudanese stuffed pittas (serves 4)

4 pitta breads

shredded lettuce

tomato slices

chopped fresh parsley

bean mixture

8oz/225g cooked red kidney beans

4oz/100g tomato, skinned and chopped

1 medium red onion, peeled and finely chopped

1 red chilli, deseeded and finely chopped

1 garlic clove, crushed

½ teaspoon ground cumin

½ teaspoon ground coriander

2 tablespoons lemon juice

1 tablespoon groundnut oil

black pepper

Fry the onion in the oil until softened, then add the remaining ingredients for the bean mixture and stir well. Cook gently, stirring frequently and mashing the beans with the back of the spoon, for about 10 minutes until the mixture is thick.

Warm the pitta breads and split them open. Fill each one with a little shredded lettuce and some of the bean mixture and garnish with tomato slices and chopped parsley.

Fried yam and green banana balls (makes 12)

12oz/350g yam, peeled and diced

8oz/225g green bananas, peeled and chopped

1 small onion, peeled and grated

1 garlic clove, crushed

1 small red chilli, deseeded and finely chopped

1 rounded tablespoon finely chopped fresh coriander

black pepper

cornmeal

groundnut oil

Steam the yam and the green bananas until tender, then mash smooth. Add the onion, garlic, chilli and coriander and season with black pepper. Mix thoroughly, take rounded dessertspoonfuls of the mixture and roll into balls. Dip these in water, then roll them in cornmeal until completely covered. Fry the balls in hot oil for a few minutes until golden, drain on kitchen paper and serve warm.

Spiced chickpea spread (serves 4)

8oz/225g cooked chickpeas, mashed

2 garlic cloves, crushed

2 tablespoons lemon juice

1 tablespoon water

1 tablespoon groundnut oil

1 rounded teaspoon ground cumin

¼ teaspoon cayenne pepper

black pepper

Mix all the ingredients until smooth and spread onto bread.

Dabo kolo (serves 4)

6oz/175g plain flour

1 rounded teaspoon brown sugar

1 rounded teaspoon berbere (see page 17)

2 tablespoons groundnut oil

cold water

extra groundnut oil

Mix the flour with the sugar and the berbere. Stir in the two tablespoonfuls of oil and gradually add enough cold water to make a soft dough. Knead the dough well, then roll it out thinly on a floured board and cut it into ½ inch/1cm diagonal pieces. Brush a heavy-based pan with oil and heat until hot. Put in the dough pieces and cook over a medium heat for a couple of minutes on each side until browned. Alternatively, place the dough pieces on an oiled baking sheet and bake in a preheated oven at 180°C/350°F/Gas mark 4 for 8-10 minutes. Allow to cool slightly before serving.

Cassava crisps (serves 4)

8oz/225g cassava

groundnut oil

paprika or chilli powder

Peel and finely slice the cassava, then soak in cold water for 15 minutes, drain and rinse. Dry the slices on a cloth or kitchen paper and fry them in hot vegetable oil until golden brown. Drain on kitchen paper and sprinkle with paprika or chilli powder.

Grilled marinated vegetables (serves 4)

Other vegetables that can be cooked in this way include yam, pumpkin, plan-tain, mushrooms and aubergine. Harder vegetables need to be part-cooked by boiling for 5 minutes before marinating.

1 corncob, cut into 1 inch/2.5cm slices

6oz/175g courgettes, thickly sliced

6oz/175g sweet potatoes, peeled and cut into chunks

4oz/100g red pepper, roughly chopped

1 medium red onion, peeled and cut into chunks

1 tomato, cut into wedges

   marinade

1 rounded tablespoon tomato purée

1 tablespoon lemon juice

1 tablespoon groundnut oil

2 tablespoons water

1 small red onion, peeled and grated

2 garlic cloves, crushed

1 inch/2.5cm piece of root ginger, grated

1 small red chilli, deseeded and finely chopped

¼ teaspoon ground cinnamon

black pepper

Boil the potato for 5 minutes, drain and put in a large bowl with the rest of the vegetables. Mix all the marinade ingredients together, then add to the vegetables and combine thoroughly. Cover and leave to marinate in the fridge for about 4 hours. Thread the vegetables onto 8 small skewers and place them on a greased baking sheet. Cook under a medium hot grill for about 15-20 minutes, turning occasionally, until tender.

Spiced nuts (serves 4)

2oz/50g cashew nuts, halved

2oz/50g peanuts, halved

1 dessertspoon groundnut oil

¼ teaspoon turmeric

¼ teaspoon cayenne pepper

¼ teaspoon ground cumin

Fry the spices in the oil for a few seconds. Add the nuts and fry, stirring frequently, until golden. Transfer to a bowl and allow to cool.

Stuffed tomatoes (serves 4)

4 large tomatoes

1oz/25g long grain rice

¼oz/7g natural minced textured vegetable protein

1 small onion, peeled and finely chopped

1 garlic clove, crushed

1 tablespoon raisins

1 dessertspoon groundnut oil

1 teaspoon tomato purée

4 fl.oz/125ml water

½ teaspoon cumin seed

¼ teaspoon paprika

black pepper

Slice the top off the tomatoes, scoop out the centres and keep these. Heat the oil in a pan and fry the onion and garlic until softened. Add the rice, cumin seed and paprika and stir around for a few seconds, then stir in the tomato centres, vegetable protein, raisins, water and tomato purée and season with black pepper. Bring to the boil, cover and simmer gently until the liquid has been absorbed. Fill each tomato with some of the mixture and put the tops back on. Arrange the tomatoes in a baking dish and bake in a preheated oven at 180°C/350°F/Gas mark 4 for 20-25 minutes until just tender.

Roasted corncobs (serves 4)

4 fresh corncobs

groundnut oil

lime juice

chilli powder

Remove the husks and threads from the corncobs and put them in a large pan of cold water. Leave to soak for 30 minutes, then pat dry on kitchen paper. Brush the cobs lightly with oil and cook them under a medium hot grill or on a barbecue, turning occasionally, for about 15 minutes until done. Sprinkle with lime juice and chilli powder before serving.

Millet pancakes (makes 6)

3oz/75g millet flour

2oz/50g plain flour

8 fl.oz/225ml warm water

groundnut oil

Whisk the two flours with the water until smooth, leave to stand for 1 hour and then whisk the mixture again. Brush a 6 inch/15cm non-stick frying pan with oil and heat until very hot. Remove from the heat, put in 2½ table-spoonfuls of batter and swirl this around to cover the base of the pan. Return the pan to the stove and cook over a high heat for about 2 minutes until golden brown underneath. Carefully turn the pancake over and cook the other side for about 2 minutes to brown. Repeat with the remaining batter to make 6 pancakes. Serve warm as an accompaniment for soups or stews or add a savoury topping and serve as a snack.

Kenyan kunde (serves 4)

8oz/225g tomatoes, skinned and chopped

8oz/225g cooked blackeye beans

4oz/100g peanuts, ground and roasted

1 onion, peeled and finely chopped

1 green chilli, deseeded and finely chopped

1 tablespoon groundnut oil

1 tablespoon tomato purée

4 tablespoons water

black pepper

chopped fresh parsley

Fry the onion and chilli in the oil until soft. Add the tomatoes, beans and tomato purée and simmer for 5 minutes, stirring frequently. Remove from the heat and mash until smooth, then add the peanuts and water and season with black pepper. Mix thoroughly, return to the heat and cook for a couple of minutes whilst stirring until the mixture is thick. Transfer to a serving dish, garnish with chopped parsley and serve with bread.

Peanut and yam patties (makes 10)

1lb/450g yam, peeled and chopped

4oz/100g peanuts, ground

1 small onion, peeled and grated

1 garlic clove, crushed

1 teaspoon cayenne pepper

groundnut oil

Boil the yam until tender, then drain and mash. Add the grated onion and garlic and 1oz/25g of the ground peanuts and combine well. Mix the remaining ground peanuts with the cayenne pepper in a mixing bowl. Take rounded tablespoonfuls of the yam mixture and roll into balls in the palm of the hand.

Dip the balls briefly in water, then roll them in the ground peanuts until completely covered. Flatten each ball slightly and shallow fry them for a few minutes on each side in hot oil until golden brown. Drain on kitchen paper and serve hot.

Ethiopian red lentils (serves 4)

8oz/225g red lentils

1 red onion, peeled and finely chopped

2 garlic cloves, crushed

1 red chilli, deseeded and finely chopped

1 dessertspoon groundnut oil

1 rounded tablespoon tomato purée

1 teaspoon paprika

½ teaspoon ground ginger

black pepper

20 fl.oz/600ml vegetable stock or water

Soften the onion, garlic and chilli in the oil, then add the remaining ingredients and stir well. Bring to the boil, cover and simmer gently, stirring frequently, for 20-25 minutes until the mixture is thick. Serve warm with bread.

Boiled millet dumplings (makes 12)

3oz/75g millet flour

3oz/75g self raising flour

2 tablespoons groundnut oil

water

Mix the two flours in a bowl and stir in the oil. Add enough water to bind, then knead the dough well and divide it into 12 equal portions. Shape each one into a small ball. Bring a pan of water to the boil, add the dumplings and boil them for 5 minutes. Add the cooked dumplings to bowls of soup.

Peanut koftas (makes 12)

6oz/175g green bananas, peeled and chopped

2oz/50g peanuts, ground and roasted

2oz/50g natural minced textured vegetable protein

2oz/50g rice flour

1 small onion, peeled and grated

1 garlic clove, crushed

1 teaspoon curry powder

½ teaspoon ground cumin

½ teaspoon ground ginger

black pepper

8 fl.oz/225ml vegetable stock

2 fl.oz/50ml water

groundnut oil

Put the vegetable protein, curry powder, cumin, ginger and vegetable stock in a small pan and bring to the boil. Cover and simmer, stirring occasionally, for about 5 minutes until the liquid has been absorbed. Remove from the heat and add the onion, garlic and peanuts.

Bring the green bananas and water to the boil in a small pan and simmer for about 5 minutes until the liquid has been absorbed. Remove from the heat and mash the banana, then add it to the peanut mixture together with the rice flour. Season with black pepper and combine well. Take rounded tablespoonfuls of the mixture and roll into balls. Fry these in hot oil for a few minutes until browned, drain on kitchen paper and serve warm with a relish or a sauce.

Fried plantain chips (serves 4)

1 large green plantain

groundnut oil

cayenne pepper

Peel and finely slice the plantain, then fry the slices for a few minutes in hot oil until golden. Drain on kitchen paper and spinkle with cayenne pepper.

MAIN COURSES

Colourful, richly-flavoured stews and curries made from nourishing combinations of lentils, beans and peas and fresh seasonal vegetables and fruits form the mainstay of the diet for many East Africans. Similar dishes are found across the region and they are very often enriched and thickened with ground and roasted nuts, especially in Ethiopia where peanuts are a favourite ingredient.

Stews and curries are always served with a starchy accompaniment such as ugali, millet or rice. Bread is often served with the main course and used to mop up any remaining sauce.

Ethiopian aubergine and lentil stew (serves 4)

1½lb/675g aubergines, diced

8oz/225g red lentils

8oz/225g tomatoes, skinned and chopped

1 large red onion, peeled and chopped

1 inch/2.5cm piece of root ginger, finely chopped

4 garlic cloves, crushed

4 tablespoons groundnut oil

1 rounded tablespoon tomato purée

2 rounded teaspoons berbere (see page 17)

25 fl.oz/750ml vegetable stock or water

finely chopped fresh coriander

Gently fry the aubergine, onion, ginger and garlic in the oil in a large pan, stirring frequently, for 10 minutes. Add the berbere and stir around for 30 seconds. Put in the tomatoes, lentils, tomato purée and stock, combine well and bring to the boil. Cover and simmer gently for about 25 minutes, stirring frequently to prevent sticking, until the vegetables are done and the stew is thick. Garnish with chopped coriander.

Mixed gingered vegetables with coconut (serves 4)

12oz/350g potatoes, peeled and thinly sliced

12oz/350g carrots, scraped and thinly sliced

12oz/350g green beans, topped, tailed and cut into 1 inch/2.5cm lengths

8oz/225g red peppers, sliced

1 red onion, peeled and sliced

2 green chillies, deseeded and finely chopped

2 inch/5cm piece of root ginger, finely chopped

2 garlic cloves, crushed

2 tablespoons groundnut oil

10 fl.oz/300ml vegetable stock or water

black pepper

2oz/50g creamed coconut, grated

Fry the onion, potatoes and carrots in a large pan in the oil for 5 minutes, stirring frequently to prevent sticking. Add the remaining ingredients apart from the coconut and stir well. Bring to the boil, cover and simmer for about 20 minutes until the vegetables are tender. Add the coconut and stir around for a minute or two until it dissolves before serving.

Fruity yam curry (serves 4)

2lb/900g yam, peeled and diced

12oz/350g green bananas, peeled and chopped

6oz/175g apples, peeled, cored and chopped

1oz/25g raisins

1 onion, peeled and chopped

1 red chilli, deseeded and finely chopped

2 inch/5cm piece of root ginger, finely chopped

2 garlic cloves, crushed

1 dessertspoon groundnut oil

2 rounded teaspoons ground coriander

2 rounded teaspoons ground cumin

½ teaspoon turmeric

½ teaspoon ground cinnamon

¼ teaspoon ground cardamom

black pepper

18 fl.oz/550ml water

finely chopped fresh coriander

Fry the onion, chilli, ginger and garlic in the oil until softened. Add the spices and stir around for 30 seconds, then add the remaining ingredients except the coriander and bring to the boil. Cover and simmer, stirring frequently, for 20-25 minutes until the curry is cooked and thick. Serve garnished with chopped coriander.

Kenyan dengu (serves 4)

12oz/350g green lentils

8oz/225g green peppers, chopped

1 green chilli, deseeded and finely chopped

1 garlic clove, crushed

1 onion, peeled and finely chopped

1 tablespoon groundnut oil

1 rounded teaspoon curry powder

black pepper

8 fl.oz/225ml coconut milk

finely chopped fresh parsley

Cook the lentils, then drain and mash. Soften the green peppers, chilli, garlic and onion in the oil, add the curry powder, mashed lentils and coconut milk and season with black pepper. Mix well, then bring to the boil, cover and simmer gently, stirring frequently, for about 10 minutes until the mixture is thick. Garnish with chopped parsley.

Peanut and vegetable wat (serves 4)

1lb/450g butternut squash, peeled, deseeded and diced

8oz/225g courgettes, chopped

8oz/225g aubergine, diced

8oz/225g green beans, topped, tailed and cut into 1 inch/2.5cm lengths

8oz/225g okras, topped, tailed and cut into diagonal slices

1 onion, peeled and finely chopped

2 garlic cloves, crushed

1 inch/2.5cm piece of root ginger, finely chopped

2oz/50g peanuts, ground and roasted

1 rounded tablespoon peanut butter

2 rounded tablespoons finely chopped fresh coriander

1 rounded dessertspoon tamarind purée

2 tablespoons groundnut oil

20 fl.oz/600ml vegetable stock or water

1 rounded teaspoon berbere (see page 17)

1 rounded teaspoon turmeric

black pepper

roasted chopped peanuts

Fry the onion, garlic, ginger and aubergine in the oil in a large pan until soft-ened. Add the berbere and turmeric and stir around for a few seconds, then put in the remaining vegetables, coriander, tamarind purée and stock and season with black pepper. Stir well, bring to the boil, cover and simmer for 15 minutes, stirring occasionally. Add the peanut butter and ground peanuts and stir until well combined. Continue simmering while stirring for a couple of minutes until the vegetables are tender and the mixture has thickened. Transfer to a serving dish and garnish with chopped peanuts.

Sweet pepper and corn stew (serves 4)

1½lb/675g mixed peppers, sliced

12oz/350g tomatoes, skinned and chopped

3 corncobs

1 red onion, peeled and sliced

1 red chilli, deseeded and finely chopped

2 garlic cloves, crushed

1 rounded dessertspoon ground cumin

1 teaspoon turmeric

2 tablespoons groundnut oil

black pepper

5 fl.oz/150ml vegetable stock or water

finely chopped fresh parsley

Fry the peppers, onion, chilli and garlic in the oil for 10 minutes, stirring frequently to prevent sticking. Cut the kernels from the corncobs and add to the pan together with the tomatoes, cumin, turmeric and stock. Season with black pepper and stir well, then raise the heat and simmer for about 10 minutes, stirring frequently, until cooked and thick. Serve sprinkled with chopped parsley.

Curried aubergine with kidney beans (serves 4)

1½lb/675g aubergines, diced

1lb/450g tomatoes, skinned and chopped

8oz/225g cooked kidney beans

2oz/50g peanuts, ground and roasted

1 onion, peeled and finely chopped

4 garlic cloves, crushed

1 red chilli, deseeded and finely chopped

1 inch/2.5cm piece of root ginger, finely chopped

4 tablespoons groundnut oil

2 rounded tablespoons finely chopped fresh coriander

1 rounded dessertspoon curry powder

8 cardamoms, husked

1 rounded teaspoon coriander seeds

1 inch/2.5cm piece of cinnamon stick

black pepper

4 tablespoons water

roasted chopped peanuts

Fry the aubergines and onion in the oil for 15 minutes, stirring frequently to prevent sticking. Grind the cardamom seeds, coriander seeds and cinnamon stick and add to the pan together with the curry powder, garlic, chilli and ginger. Stir around for 1 minute, then add the tomatoes, water and fresh coriander and simmer for 10 minutes while stirring occasionally. Put in the beans and ground peanuts and season with black pepper and, stirring all the time, continue simmering for a few minutes until the mixture thickens. Garnish with chopped peanuts.

Root vegetable and lentil awaze (serves 4)

1½lb/675g mixed root vegetables (e.g. potato, sweet potato, yam, carrot), peeled and diced

1 quantity of awaze (see page 86)

4oz/100g brown lentils

1 large red onion, peeled and finely chopped

2 garlic cloves, crushed

1 tablespoon groundnut oil

finely chopped fresh coriander

Put the lentils in a pan of water and bring to the boil. Cover and simmer for 30 minutes, then drain over a bowl and keep the cooking liquid. Fry the onion and garlic in the oil in a large pan until soft. Make the cooking liquid up to 12 fl.oz/350ml if necessary with water and add to the pan together with the root vegetables. Bring to the boil, cover and simmer, stirring occasionally, for 10 minutes. Add the lentils and awaze and mix thoroughly. Bring back to the boil, then cover and simmer, stirring frequently, for about 10 minutes until the mixture is cooked and thick. Sprinkle with chopped coriander before serving.

Spinach, potato and chickpea stew (serves 4)

12oz/350g fresh spinach, shredded

12oz/350g potatoes, peeled and finely diced

8oz/225g tomatoes, skinned and chopped

8oz/225g cooked chickpeas

1 onion, peeled and chopped

1 green chilli, deseeded and finely chopped

2 garlic cloves, crushed

1 tablespoon groundnut oil

1 rounded teaspoon ground cumin

black pepper

5 fl.oz/150ml water

Heat the oil in a large pan and fry the onion, garlic and chilli for a few minutes, then add the tomatoes, potatoes, ground cumin and water and bring to the boil. Cover and simmer, stirring frequently, for 10 minutes. Put in the spinach and chickpeas, season with black pepper and continue cooking for about 15 minutes, stirring frequently to prevent sticking, until the vegetables are tender and the mixture is thick.

Sweet potato, plantain and blackeye bean stew (serves 4)

1½lb/675g sweet potatoes, peeled and diced

1lb/450g unripe plantains, peeled and chopped

10oz/300g cooked blackeye beans

1 onion, peeled and chopped

2 garlic cloves, crushed

1 dessertspoon groundnut oil

2 teaspoons ground coriander

2 teaspoons ground cumin

1 teaspoon turmeric

½ teaspoon cayenne pepper

24 fl.oz/725ml vegetable stock

1oz/25g creamed coconut, grated

finely chopped fresh coriander

Fry the onion and garlic in the oil in a large pan until softened. Add the spices and stir around for a few seconds, then add the sweet potato, plantain and stock and stir well. Bring to the boil, cover and simmer, stirring frequently, for about 15 minutes until tender. Stir in the coconut and beans and continue simmering for a couple of minutes. Serve garnished with chopped coriander.

Spicy squash and chickpea stew (serves 4)

2½lb/1.1kg butternut squash, peeled, deseeded and diced

8oz/225g cooked chickpeas

8oz/225g tomatoes, skinned and chopped

8oz/225g red pepper, chopped

1oz/25g raisins

1 red onion, peeled and chopped

1 red chilli, deseeded and finely chopped

2 garlic cloves, crushed

12 fl.oz/350ml vegetable stock or water

1 tablespoon vegetable oil

1 dessertspoon ground cumin

1 teaspoon ground ginger

½ teaspoon turmeric

6 cardamoms, husked and the seeds separated

black pepper

finely chopped fresh parsley

Heat the oil in a large pan and fry the onion until softened. Add the spices and tomatoes and stir around for 1 minute, then put in the remaining ingredients apart from the parsley and stir well. Bring to the boil, cover and simmer, stirring occasionally, for about 20 minutes until the mixture is thick and cooked. Garnish with fresh parsley.

Spinach with peppers and lentils (serves 4)

1lb/450g fresh spinach, shredded

12oz/350g mixed peppers, chopped

8oz/225g green lentils

1 onion, peeled and chopped

1 green chilli, deseeded and finely chopped

2 garlic cloves, crushed

1 tablespoon groundnut oil

2 rounded tablespoons finely chopped fresh coriander

2 rounded teaspoons ground cumin

1 rounded teaspoon ground coriander

1 rounded teaspoon turmeric

black pepper

Put the lentils in a large pan of water and bring to the boil. Simmer until tender, then drain over a bowl and keep the cooking liquid, making it up to 10 fl.oz/300ml with water if necessary. Fry the peppers, onion and chilli in the oil until soft, add the spinach and cook gently until it wilts. Stir in the lentils, garlic, coriander, spices and the measured cooking liquid and bring to the boil. Cover and simmer, stirring occasionally, for 10-15 minutes until the vegetables are done and the mixture is thick.

Aubergine, chickpea and cashew nut curry (serves 4)

1½lb/675g aubergines, diced

8oz/225g cooked chickpeas

4oz/100g green pepper, chopped

4oz/100g red pepper, chopped

4oz/100g tomato, skinned and chopped

2oz/50g cashew nuts, ground and roasted

1 red onion, peeled and finely chopped

2 garlic cloves, crushed

1 red chilli, deseeded and finely chopped

4 tablespoons groundnut oil

8 fl.oz/225ml vegetable stock or water

2 rounded teaspoons curry powder

1 teaspoon turmeric

1 teaspoon ground ginger

6 cardamoms, husked and the seeds separated

black pepper

roasted cashew nuts

Fry the aubergine, onion, garlic and chilli in the oil, stirring frequently, for 10 minutes. Put in the spices and stir around for a few seconds, then add the green and red pepper, tomato and stock. Bring to the boil, cover and simmer, stirring occasionally, for 10 minutes. Add the chickpeas and continue cooking for a few minutes more until the vegetables are tender. Stir in the ground cashew nuts and stir for a minute or so until well combined. Sprinkle with roasted cashew nuts when serving.

GRAINS

For many East Africans living in poor and remote villages ugali is the subsistence food, around which all meals are based. Dried maize is pounded to a meal in a mortar with a pestle and then cooked in water to make a stiff porridge-type mixture. This is rolled into a hollowed-out ball in the fingers and used to scoop up stews. A thinner version known as uji is eaten for breakfast.

Millet and sorghum are widely grown across the region and both these crops are resistant to drought. They are mainly served plainly cooked. Unfortunately sorghum, which is a native wild plant, is not readily obtainable outside Africa. Barley is a staple crop in Ethiopia and this is also served plainly cooked, as an accompaniment for stews, although it is sometimes combined with green leafy vegetables.

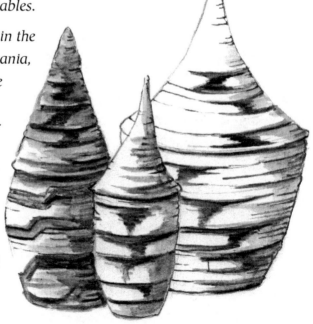

Rice, a major crop in the Sudan and in Tanzania, is served in large quantities as an accompaniment for curries and stews, or mixed with other ingredients to make flavourful biriani and pilau dishes which can be served with bread as light meals.

Ugali (serves 4)

8oz/225g cornmeal

30 fl.oz/900ml water

Put the water in a large pan and bring to the boil. Remove from the heat and gradually add the cornmeal, whisking all the time until smooth. Cook over a medium heat, stirring constantly, for 10 minutes until the mixture is thick and smooth. But be careful when cooking, as the ugali tends to spit out of the pan when the heat is turned up too high.

Millet with corn (serves 4)

8oz/225g millet

1 corncob

1 onion, peeled and finely chopped

1 tablespoon groundnut oil

1 teaspoon cumin seeds

½ teaspoon turmeric

black pepper

24 fl.oz/725ml water

Fry the onion in the oil until softened. Cut the kernels from the cob and add to the pan, with the millet, cumin and turmeric. Stir around for a minute or two, then pour in the water and season with black pepper. Bring to the boil, cover and simmer gently for 15-20 minutes until the liquid has been absorbed.

Barley with spinach (serves 4)

12oz/350g fresh spinach, finely shredded

8oz/225g pot barley

1 onion, peeled and chopped

1 green chilli, deseeded and finely chopped

1 teaspoon cumin seeds

1 dessertspoon groundnut oil

black pepper

chopped fresh parsley

Soak the barley in boiling water for 1 hour. Drain, bring to the boil in fresh water, cover and simmer for 20 minutes. Drain over a bowl and keep the cooking liquid. Heat the oil in a large pan and fry the onion and chilli until soft. Add the cumin seeds and stir around for 30 seconds, then put in the spinach and cook until it wilts. Add the barley and 10 fl.oz/300ml of the cooking liquid and season with black pepper. Bring to the boil and simmer, stirring frequently, for 10 minutes. Sprinkle with chopped parsley when serving.

Fried spiced peanut rice (serves 4)

8oz/225g long grain rice

3oz/75g peanuts, finely chopped and roasted

1 onion, peeled and finely chopped

2 tablespoons groundnut oil

1 teaspoon cumin seeds

1 inch/2.5cm piece of cinnamon stick, crumbled

½ teaspoon turmeric

black pepper

Cook the rice, drain and rinse. Spread it out on a plate and leave for a few hours to dry. Fry the onion in the oil until soft. Add the cumin seeds, cinnamon and turmeric and stir around for 30 seconds, then add the rice and season with black pepper and stir around for a couple of minutes until heated through. Mix in the peanuts before serving.

Yellow coconut rice (serves 4)

12oz/350g long grain rice

2oz/50g creamed coconut, grated

1 onion, peeled and finely chopped

1 tablespoon groundnut oil

½ teaspoon turmeric

black pepper

30 fl.oz/900ml water

toasted flaked coconut

Soften the onion in the oil, then put in the turmeric and rice and stir around for 1 minute. Add the creamed coconut and water and season with black pepper, stir well and bring to the boil. Cover and simmer gently until the liquid has been absorbed and the rice is done. Transfer to a serving dish and fork through before garnishing with toasted flaked coconut.

Tanzanian rice with vegetables (serves 4)

8oz/225g long grain rice

8oz/225g carrots, scraped and finely chopped

8oz/225g green beans, topped, tailed and cut into ½ inch/1cm lengths

4oz/100g sweetcorn kernels

1 onion, peeled and finely chopped

2 garlic cloves, crushed

1 red chilli, deseeded and finely chopped

1 tablespoon groundnut oil

24 fl.oz/725ml vegetable stock or water

½ teaspoon turmeric

6 cloves

black pepper

finely chopped fresh coriander

Fry the onion in the oil until softened. Add the turmeric, chilli and rice and stir around for 1 minute, then the remaining ingredients and combine well. Bring to the boil, cover and simmer gently until the liquid has been absorbed. Sprinkle with chopped coriander before serving.

Zanzibari fruit pilau (serves 4)

8oz/225g basmati rice

8oz/225g eating apples, peeled, cored and finely chopped

1oz/25g raisins

1 onion, peeled and finely chopped

1 inch/2.5cm piece of root ginger, finely chopped

1 tablespoon groundnut oil

2 inch/5cm piece of cinnamon stick

1 teaspoon cumin seeds

8 cloves

½ teaspoon turmeric

20 fl.oz/600ml water

toasted cashew nuts

Heat the oil and soften the onion and ginger. Add the rice and spices and stir around for 1 minute. Now add the apple, raisins and water and stir well. Bring to the boil, cover and simmer gently until the liquid has been absorbed. Serve garnished with toasted cashew nuts.

Rice and lentils (serves 4)

8oz/225g long grain rice

8oz/225g brown lentils

1 onion, peeled and finely chopped

2 garlic cloves, crushed

1 tablespoon groundnut oil

2 teaspoons cumin seeds

black pepper

24 fl.oz/725ml vegetable stock or water

½oz/15g creamed coconut, grated

Bring the lentils to the boil in a large pan of water, cover and simmer for 30 minutes, then drain. Fry the onion and garlic in the oil until soft, put in the rice and cumin seeds and stir around for 1 minute. Add the lentils and vegetable stock and season with black pepper. Bring to the boil, cover and simmer until the liquid has been absorbed. Stir in the grated coconut until it dissolves before serving.

Pineapple and vegetable biriani (serves 4)

8oz/225g long grain rice

8oz/225g tin pineapple slices in natural juice

4oz/100g sweetcorn kernels

4oz/100g green beans, topped, tailed and cut into 1 inch/2.5cm lengths

4oz/100g red pepper, chopped

4oz/100g green pepper, chopped

1oz/25g raisins

1 tablespoon groundnut oil

1 onion, peeled and finely chopped

1 small red chilli, deseeded and finely chopped

1 inch/2.5cm piece of root ginger, finely chopped

2 garlic cloves, crushed

1 inch/2.5cm piece of cinnamon stick

1 teaspoon fenugreek seeds

½ teaspoon coriander seeds

½ teaspoon turmeric

6 cardamom pods, husked and the seeds separated

6 cloves

black pepper

18 fl.oz/525ml vegetable stock or water

roasted cashew nuts

In a large pan fry the onion, chilli, ginger and garlic until softened in the oil. Add the spices and rice and stir around for 1 minute. Strain the pineapple juice into the pan. Finely chop the pineapple slices and add these together with the remaining ingredients apart from the cashew nuts. Stir well and bring to the boil, then cover and simmer gently until the liquid has been absorbed. Transfer to a serving dish and garnish with roasted cashews.

Tomato and pea pilau rice (serves 4)

8oz/225g long grain rice

8oz/225g tomatoes, skinned and finely chopped

8oz/225g shelled peas

1 green chilli, deseeded and finely chopped

1 onion, peeled and finely chopped

2 garlic cloves, crushed

20 fl.oz/600ml water

2 tablespoons finely chopped fresh coriander

1 dessertspoon groundnut oil

1 teaspoon cumin seeds

1 teaspoon paprika

black pepper

tomato wedges

green chilli rings

Heat the oil and fry the onion until soft. Add the chopped tomatoes and chilli, garlic, cumin seeds and paprika and stir around for a couple of minutes. Put in the rice, peas, water and coriander and season with black pepper, stir well and bring to the boil. Cover and simmer gently until the liquid has been absorbed and the rice is done. Spoon into a serving dish and garnish with tomato wedges and chilli rings.

VEGETABLES

All kinds of starchy vegetables such as cassava, eddo, potato, sweet potato and yam are simply boiled and mashed and served with soups and stews. Plantains and green bananas are also treated as vegetables and are either boiled or steamed in their skins and then peeled and mashed and served on their own, or combined with other mashed vegetables.

Irio, mashed potato and peas with sweetcorn, is a traditional Kenyan dish. It is commonly served shaped into a mound with a hollowed-out centre, which is filled with a savoury such as a relish or a contrasting vegetable dish such as kale with tomatoes, braised cabbage with coconut, spicy coconut spinach or green beans with chickpeas. Many vegetable dishes are prepared in the same way throughout the region, with different ingredients being used according to what's available or in season. This is particularly so with green leafy vegetables, many varieties of which are harvested from the wild. All the dishes are quick and easy to make and a couple of contrasting vegetable dishes served with a grain dish and bread makes a colourful and appetising main course meal.

Irio (serves 4)

1½lb/675g potatoes, peeled and diced

8oz/225g shelled peas

1 corncob

1 tablespoon groundnut oil

1 onion, peeled and finely chopped

black pepper

Put the potatoes and peas in a pan and just cover with water. Bring to the boil, cover and simmer until done, then drain and keep 4 tablespoonfuls of the cooking liquid. Mash the potatoes and peas smooth. Cut the kernels from the corncob and blanch for a couple of minutes until tender, then drain. Fry the onion in the oil until soft and add the mashed potatoes and peas together with the sweetcorn and cooking liquid. Season with black pepper, mix until well combined and keep stirring over a low heat until heated through before serving.

Kale with tomatoes (serves 4)

1lb/450g kale

12oz/350g tomatoes, skinned and finely chopped

1 onion, peeled and finely chopped

2 tablespoons groundnut oil

2 tablespoons water

1 teaspoon cumin seeds

black pepper

Remove the thick stalks from the kale and finely shred the leaves. Fry the onion in the oil in a large pan until soft, then add the cumin seeds and stir for a few seconds. Add the kale, tomatoes and water and season with black pepper. Stir well, then cover and cook for about 20 minutes, stirring occasionally, until tender.

Spiced squash purée (serves 4)

2lb/900g butternut squash, peeled, deseeded and diced

1 onion, peeled and finely chopped

1 dessertspoon groundnut oil

1 teaspoon ground cumin

1 teaspoon ground coriander

black pepper

Soften the onion in the oil. Steam the squash until done, then add it to the onion together with the spices. Stir around for 1 minute, remove from the heat and mash to a purée.

Sweet potato with peanut sauce (serves 4)

1½lb/675g sweet potatoes, peeled and diced

1 red onion, peeled and finely chopped

1 inch/2.5cm piece of root ginger, finely chopped

3oz/75g peanuts

1 dessertspoon groundnut oil

9 fl.oz/250ml water

1 rounded teaspoon berbere (see page 17)

Dry roast the peanuts in a heavy-based pan until golden. Chop and keep a few for garnish and grind the rest.

Fry the onion and ginger in the oil until soft, then add the berbere and stir around for a few seconds. Put in the sweet potatoes and the water and stir well. Bring to the boil, cover and simmer, stirring occasionally, for about 10 minutes until cooked. Add the ground peanuts and mix thoroughly. Continue simmering for a couple of minutes until the mixture is thick, then garnish with the chopped peanuts before serving.

Yam chips (serves 4)

1½lb/675g yam, peeled and cut into chips
groundnut oil
lemon juice
chilli powder

Put the yam chips in a pan of boiling water and simmer for 5 minutes. Drain and pat dry on a cloth or on kitchen paper, then fry the chips in hot oil until golden. Drain on kitchen paper and sprinkle with lemon juice and chilli powder.

Braised cabbage with coconut (serves 4)

12oz/350g green cabbage
1 onion, peeled and finely sliced
2 garlic cloves, crushed
2 dessertspoons groundnut oil
8 fl.oz/225ml vegetable stock or water
1oz/25g creamed coconut, grated
black pepper

Cut the thick stalks from the cabbage and finely shred the leaves. Fry the cabbage, onion and garlic for 5 minutes in the oil in a large pan, stirring frequently until the cabbage has wilted. Add the stock and season with black pepper. Simmer for about 10 minutes, stirring occasionally, until cooked, then add the coconut and stir around until it dissolves before serving.

Fufu (serves 4)

1½lb/675g yam or cassava or sweet potato, peeled and cut into chunks
1 tablespoon vegan margarine
black pepper

Cook the yam, cassava or sweet potato, drain and mash with the margarine until smooth. Season with black pepper, then take rounded dessertspoonfuls of the mixture and roll into balls. Serve warm as an accompaniment to soups and stews.

Red kidney beans with corn (serves 4)

8oz/225g cooked red kidney beans

8oz/225g sweetcorn kernels

1 red onion, peeled and finely chopped

2 garlic cloves, crushed

1 dessertspoon groundnut oil

5 fl.oz/150ml vegetable stock or water

black pepper

finely chopped fresh parsley

Fry the onion and garlic in the oil until soft. Add the kidney beans, sweetcorn and vegetable stock and season with black pepper. Bring to the boil, cover and simmer, stirring occasionally, for 5 minutes. Transfer to a serving dish and sprinkle with chopped parsley.

Pumpkin with tomato and tamarind sauce (serves 4)

1lb/450g pumpkin, peeled and diced

6oz/175g tomatoes, skinned and chopped

1 red onion, peeled and finely chopped

1 garlic clove, crushed

1 tablespoon tamarind purée

1 tablespoon water

1 tablespoon lemon juice

1 dessertspoon groundnut oil

½ teaspoon paprika

black pepper

finely chopped fresh parsley

Heat the oil in a large pan and fry the onion and garlic until softened. Add the remaining ingredients except the parsley and mix well. Bring to the boil, cover and simmer, stirring frequently, for about 15-20 minutes until tender. Garnish with chopped parsley before serving.

Matoke (serves 4)

2lb/900g unripe plantains, peeled and chopped

1 onion, peeled and finely chopped

1 tablespoon groundnut oil

2 tablespoons lemon juice

28 fl.oz/825ml vegetable stock or water

¼ teaspoon cayenne pepper

black pepper

Soften the onion in the oil, then add the remaining ingredients and stir well. Bring to the boil, cover and simmer, stirring frequently, for about 20 minutes until the liquid has been absorbed and the plantain is done. Remove from the heat and mash smooth and serve as an accompaniment for stews.

Spicy coconut spinach (serves 4)

1lb/450g fresh spinach, finely shredded

1 onion, peeled and finely chopped

2 garlic cloves, crushed

1 dessertspoon groundnut oil

1 rounded teaspoon ground cumin

1 rounded teaspoon ground coriander

black pepper

4 fl.oz/125ml coconut milk

Heat the oil in a large pan and fry the onion and garlic until soft. Add the cumin, coriander and spinach and cook for about 5 minutes until the spinach has wilted. Pour in the coconut milk, season with black pepper and simmer while stirring for 2-3 minutes until the spinach is cooked.

Green beans with chickpeas (serves 4)

8oz/225g green beans, topped, tailed and cut into 1 inch/2.5cm lengths

4oz/100g cooked chickpeas

4oz/100g tomato, skinned and chopped

1 onion, peeled and finely chopped

1 garlic clove, crushed

1 red chilli, deseeded and finely chopped

1 dessertspoon groundnut oil

1 rounded tablespoon finely chopped fresh coriander

2 tablespoons water

1 dessertspoon tamarind purée

black pepper

Heat the oil and soften the onion, garlic and chilli. Add the green beans, tomato, coriander, water and tamarind purée and season with black pepper. Simmer for 5 minutes, then add the chickpeas and continue simmering, stirring frequently, until the beans are tender.

Sweet potato and cardamom balls (serves 4)

1½lb/675g sweet potatoes, peeled

1 onion, peeled and grated

1 dessertspoon groundnut oil

½ teaspoon ground cardamom

black pepper

Cut the potatoes into chunks and boil or steam until done, meanwhile frying the onion in the oil until soft. Drain and mash the potatoes and add the onion and cardamom. Season with black pepper and mix thoroughly. Take rounded tablespoonfuls of the mixture and roll into balls before serving.

Ethiopian greens (serves 4)

1lb/450g green leafy vegetables, (e.g. kale, cabbage, spring greens, etc.)

6oz/175g green peppers, sliced

1 red onion, peeled and finely chopped

2 garlic cloves, crushed

1 green chilli, deseeded and finely chopped

1 tablespoon groundnut oil

4 fl.oz/125ml water

black pepper

Cut any thick stalks from the green leaves and discard. Steam the leaves for 5 minutes, then chop them finely.

Fry the onion and pepper in the oil until softened, add the green leaves and remaining ingredients and stir well. Simmer for about 5 minutes, adding a little more water if necessary and stirring frequently, until tender. Serve hot or cold.

Potatoes with chickpeas and peanuts (serves 4)

1½lb/675g potatoes, peeled and diced

4oz/100g cooked chickpeas

1oz/25g ground peanuts, roasted

1 onion, peeled and finely chopped

1 garlic clove, crushed

1 small red chilli, deseeded and finely chopped

1 dessertspoon groundnut oil

7 fl.oz/200ml vegetable stock or water

½ teaspoon paprika

½ teaspoon ground cumin

black pepper

finely chopped fresh coriander

Cook the potatoes and drain. Meanwhile soften the onion, garlic and chilli in the oil in a large pan. Add the paprika, ground cumin, chickpeas and stock and season with black pepper. Stir well and bring to the boil. Cover and simmer for 3 minutes, then stir in the peanuts and continue simmering for 2 minutes before adding the potatoes. Mix thoroughly, transfer to a serving dish and garnish with chopped coriander.

Spiced braised white cabbage (serves 4)

12oz/350g white cabbage, finely shredded

1 onion, peeled and finely sliced

1 small green chilli, deseeded and finely chopped

1 garlic clove, crushed

1 tablespoon groundnut oil

1 teaspoon curry powder

1 teaspoon cumin seeds

½ teaspoon ground ginger

black pepper

3 fl.oz/75ml water

Heat the oil in a large pan and fry the cabbage, onion, chilli and garlic for 5 minutes. Add the remaining ingredients and stir well. Bring to the boil, cover and simmer, stirring occasionally, for about 10 minutes until cooked.

Baked sweet potatoes with sweetcorn relish (serves 4)

4 sweet potatoes (each approx. 8oz/225g)

groundnut oil

sweetcorn relish (see page XXX)

Scrub the potatoes and brush them lightly with oil. Place them on a baking tray and cut a cross in the top of each one. Bake in a preheated oven at 200°C/400°F/Gas mark 6, turning once during cooking, for about 1 hour. Split the potatoes open and top them with some relish.

BREADS

A wide variety of interesting and flavourful speciality breads are made across the region, which are eaten throughout the day as snacks or used to mop up soups and stews. Millet is ground into a greyish flour and mixed with other flours to make various distinctively-flavoured breads. Cornbread is a particular favourite in Tanzania and flavoured chapatis are popular with curries.

Injera, a traditional Ethiopian pancake-type bread, is sometimes made with barley flour or cornmeal rather than millet flour. Instead of the more manageable size given here they are about 24 inches in diameter and baked on large flat griddles. These huge breads are placed directly on the table as a kind of edible tablecloth or plate and the other fare is spooned on top. The diners break off pieces of the bread and use them to roll or scoop up the other foods.

Ambasha

1lb/450g plain flour

½ teaspoon salt

1 rounded teaspoon easy-blend yeast

2 tablespoons groundnut oil

1 teaspoon coriander seeds

1 teaspoon fenugreek seeds

½ teaspoon cardamom seeds

¼ teaspoon white pepper

approx. 8 fl.oz/225ml warm water

to finish

1 dessertspoon groundnut oil

¼ teaspoon cayenne pepper

½ teaspoon ground ginger

Grind the coriander, fenugreek and cardamom seeds and put them in a bowl with the flour, salt, yeast and white pepper. Mix well, then stir in the 2 table-spoonfuls of oil and gradually add the warm water until a stiff dough forms. Knead the dough for 5 minutes, return it to the bowl, cover and leave in a warm place for 1 hour to rise. Knead the dough again, then break off a walnut-sized piece and roll it into a ball. Shape the rest of the dough into a round of about 7 inches/18cm diameter. Transfer to a greased baking tin, score into 8 equal wedges and put the small dough ball in the centre. Keep in a warm place for 30 minutes to rise, then lightly score through the cut lines again if necessary and bake in a preheated oven at 200°C/400°F/Gas mark 6 for 15-20 minutes until golden brown and hollow sounding when tapped underneath.

Mix the cayenne pepper and ginger with the dessertspoonful of oil and brush over the top of the warm bread. Serve warm.

Millet bread

12oz/350g plain wholemeal flour
4oz/100g millet flour
1 rounded teaspoon easy-blend yeast
½ teaspoon salt
2 tablespoons groundnut oil
approx. 9 fl.oz/250ml warm water

Mix the wholemeal flour with the millet flour, yeast and salt. Stir in the oil, then gradually add enough warm water to form a soft dough. Turn this out onto a floured board and knead well. Return the dough to the bowl, cover and leave to rise for an hour in a warm place. Knead the dough again and form it into a 6 inch/15cm diameter circle. Transfer to a greased baking tin and put in a warm place for another 30 minutes. Lightly score the top of the dough in a diagonal pattern with a sharp knife. Bake in a preheated oven at 200°C/400°F/Gas mark 6 for about 20 minutes until golden. Allow to cool slightly on a wire rack before cutting.

Cornbread

4oz/100g fine cornmeal
4oz/100g plain flour
1 rounded teaspoon easy-blend yeast
¼ teaspoon salt
2 small dried red chillies, crushed
1 tablespoon groundnut oil
10 fl.oz/300ml warm water

Mix the cornmeal with the flour, yeast, salt and crushed chillies in a large bowl. Stir in the oil, then add the water and mix until a thick batter forms. Spoon this evenly into a base-lined and greased 7 inch/18cm round baking tin and leave in a warm place for 1 hour to rise, then bake in a preheated oven at 180°C/350°F/Gas mark 4 for about 25 minutes until browned and hollow sounding when tapped underneath. Let the cornbread cool slightly before cutting and serving.

Maandazi (makes 8)

8oz/225g plain flour

½oz/15g brown sugar

1 teaspoon easy-blend yeast

¼ teaspoon salt

pinch of ground cinnamon

1 tablespoon groundnut oil

approx. 4 fl.oz/125ml warm water

extra oil

Combine the flour with the sugar, yeast, salt and cinnamon, stir in the table-spoonful of oil and then gradually add the water until a stiff dough forms. Knead the dough well, return it to the bowl and leave to rise for an hour in a warm place. Knead the dough again on a floured board and divide it into 8 equal portions. Roll each one into a flattened ball and leave them in a warm place for 30 minutes. Shallow fry the maandazi in hot oil for a few minutes on each side until golden brown. Drain on kitchen paper and serve warm.

Rice and coconut bread

4oz/100g rice flour

4oz/100g plain flour

¼ teaspoon salt

1 teaspoon easy-blend yeast

pinch of ground cardamom

1 tablespoon groundnut oil

1oz/25g creamed coconut, grated

5 fl.oz/150ml warm water

Mix the two flours with the salt, yeast and ground cardamom in a large bowl and stir in the oil. Dissolve the creamed coconut in the warm water and add to the mixture. Combine thoroughly, then turn out onto a floured board and knead well. Return the dough to the bowl, cover and put in a warm place for 40 minutes to rise. Knead the dough again, then shape it into a flattened circle and place it on a greased baking sheet. Keep in a warm place for 30 minutes. Bake in a preheated oven at 200°C/400°F/Gas mark 6 for 20-25 minutes until golden. Allow to cool slightly before cutting.

Injera (makes 4)

6oz/175g plain flour

2oz/50g millet flour

1 teaspoon easy-blend yeast

pinch of salt

12 fl.oz/350ml warm water

1 teaspoon baking powder

groundnut oil

Mix the plain flour, millet flour, yeast and salt in a large lidded bowl or saucepan. Add the water and combine well until a smooth batter forms. Cover and leave overnight.

Add the baking powder and mix thoroughly, then cover and leave for 30 minutes. Brush a 9 inch/23cm diameter non-stick frying pan with oil and heat until hot. Remove from the heat and add 4 tablespoonfuls of the batter, swirling it around to cover the base of the pan, then return to a medium heat and cook for 3-4 minutes until the underside is golden and the top is set and sponge-like in texture. Repeat with the remaining batter to make 4 breads. Injera are cooked on one side only. Lower the heat if the underside browns too much before the top sets.

Onion chapatis (makes 8)

8oz/225g plain flour
1 small onion, peeled and grated
pinch of salt
warm water
groundnut oil

Stir the flour, salt and grated onion together, then add enough warm water to make a soft dough. Turn this out onto a floured board and knead it well. Return it to the bowl, cover and leave for 30 minutes. Knead the dough again and divide it into 8 equal portions. Roll each piece into a ball and flatten these into rounds of about 5½ inches/14cm. Lightly brush each side of the dough with oil. Heat a heavy-based pan until hot and cook the chapatis for a minute or two on each side until lightly browned. Serve warm.

Coconut chapatis (makes 8)

8oz/225g plain flour
1oz/25g creamed coconut, grated
pinch of salt
5 fl.oz/150ml warm water
groundnut oil

Mix the flour with the salt in a large bowl. Dissolve the creamed coconut in the warm water, add to the bowl and combine well until a soft dough forms. Turn out onto a floured board and knead, adding more flour if necessary until the dough is no longer sticky. Divide it into 8 equal portions and roll these out on a floured board into a circle of about 5½ inches/14cm. Lightly brush the circles with oil on both sides. Heat a heavy-based pan until hot, then cook the chapatis for a couple of minutes on each side until lightly browned. Serve warm.

Steamed millet bread

8oz/225g plain wholemeal flour

4oz/100g millet flour

1 rounded teaspoon easy-blend yeast

½ teaspoon salt

approx. 8 fl.oz/225ml warm water

groundnut oil

Combine the wholemeal flour with the millet flour, yeast and salt and gradually add the warm water until a stiff dough forms. Knead the dough well, return it to the bowl and put in a warm place for 1 hour to rise. Knead the dough again on a floured board, then divide it into 8 equal portions. Brush a 7 inch/18cm rigid steamer with oil. Roll the pieces of dough into balls and arrange them in the steamer in a single layer. Leave to rise for 30 minute, then steam over a pan of boiling water for 20-25 minutes until firm to the touch. Serve warm.

SALADS

In the Sudan it is customary to serve small individual bowls of salad for each diner and these are an integral part of the main course meal. In other countries large bowls of salad are served alongside cooked dishes for diners to help themselves to.

Savoury fruit salads and those made with yoghurt are refreshing and cooling, and they are favourite accompaniments for hot spicy dishes. Red kidney bean and coconut salad is typical of the many cooked and then cooled salads enjoyed in Kenya and these are often eaten with bread, as a snack.

All the following salads are ideal for serving with snacks and some are suitable for use as fillings for pitta breads.

Aubergine salad (serves 4)

12oz/350g aubergines, finely diced

2 tablespoons groundnut oil

1 small red onion, peeled and finely chopped

1 small red chilli, deseeded and finely chopped

1 garlic clove, crushed

1 tablespoon lemon juice

black pepper

finely chopped fresh parsley

Fry the aubergines in the oil, stirring frequently, until tender. Remove from the heat and add the onion, chilli, garlic and lemon juice. Season with black pepper and toss thoroughly. Spoon into a serving dish, cover and refrigerate until cold. Garnish with chopped parsley before serving.

Ethiopian lentil salad (serves 4)

4oz/100g brown lentils

4oz/100g tomato, skinned and finely chopped

4oz/100g red pepper, finely chopped

1 small red onion, peeled and finely chopped

2 garlic cloves, crushed

1 tablespoon finely chopped fresh coriander

1 small dried red chilli, crushed

1 dessertspoon groundnut oil

1 tablespoon lemon juice

black pepper

extra chopped fresh coriander

Cook the lentils, then drain and mash them. Add the tomato, red pepper, onion, garlic and tablespoonful of coriander. Mix the oil with the lemon juice and chilli and pour over the salad, season with black pepper and combine well. Transfer to a serving dish and garnish with fresh coriander. Serve warm or cold.

Savoury fruit salad

Savoury fruit salads are popular throughout the region and are often served as an accompaniment to the main meal. Variations occur in different countries, but popular fruits included in most are pineapple, banana, orange, paw paw, mango and avocado. These are chopped and mixed with shredded lettuce and spinach leaves and drizzled with simple lemon or lime dressings. For an authentic finish, sprinkle with fresh grated coconut and roasted peanuts.

Red kidney bean and coconut salad (serves 4)

6oz/175g cooked red kidney beans

4oz/100g green pepper, chopped

4oz/100g tomato, skinned and chopped

1 medium red onion, peeled and finely chopped

1 garlic clove, crushed

1 red chilli, deseeded and finely chopped

1 dessertspoon groundnut oil

¼ teaspoon ground cardamom

black pepper

½oz/15g creamed coconut, grated

2 fl.oz/50ml water

shredded lettuce

finely chopped fresh parsley

Fry the green pepper, onion, garlic and chilli in the oil until softened. Add the tomato and stir around until pulpy. Stir in the kidney beans, cardamom, coconut and water and season with black pepper. Bring to the boil and simmer uncovered, stirring frequently, for about 10 minutes until the mixture thickens. Allow to cool, then serve on a bed of shredded lettuce, garnished with chopped parsley.

Tanzanian mixed salad (serves 4)

4oz/100g tomato

4oz/100g carrots, scraped

4oz/100g cucumber

1 medium red onion, peeled

1 small red chilli, deseeded

1 tablespoon finely chopped fresh parsley

1 dessertspoon vegetable oil

1 tablespoon lemon juice

black pepper

finely shredded lettuce

Chop the tomato, carrots, cucumber, onion and chilli very finely and put in a bowl. Mix the oil with the lemon juice and add to the salad, together with the parsley. Season with black pepper and toss thoroughly. Arrange some shredded lettuce on a serving plate and pile the salad on top.

Cucumber and yoghurt salad (serves 4)

8oz/225g cucumber, finely chopped

8 fl.oz/225ml plain soya yoghurt

1 green chilli, deseeded and finely chopped

1 garlic clove, crushed

black pepper

finely chopped fresh coriander

Mix the cucumber with the yoghurt, chilli and garlic. Season with black pepper and spoon into a serving bowl. Sprinkle with chopped coriander.

Mixed bean salad (serves 4)

8oz/225g green beans, topped, tailed and cut into ½ inch/1cm
    lengths

8oz/225g mixed cooked beans

4oz/100g tomato, skinned and finely chopped

1 small red onion, peeled and finely chopped

1 small red chilli, deseeded and finely chopped

1 garlic clove, crushed

2 rounded tablespoons finely chopped fresh coriander

1 tablespoon groundnut oil

2 tablespoons lime juice

black pepper

Steam the green beans until just tender, then rinse under cold running water. Drain well and put in a large bowl with the mixed beans, tomato, onion and coriander. Mix the oil with the lime juice, chilli and garlic and season with black pepper. Add to the salad and combine well before transferring to a serving bowl.

White cabbage and onion salad (serves 4)

8oz/225g white cabbage, finely shredded

1 medium red onion, peeled and finely sliced

1 small red chilli, deseeded and finely chopped

1 garlic clove, crushed

1 dessertspoon groundnut oil

2 dessertspoons lemon juice

2 tablespoons finely chopped fresh parsley

black pepper

Mix the cabbage and onion in a large bowl. Combine the chilli with the garlic, oil and lemon juice, then add to the salad together with the parsley. Season with black pepper and toss thoroughly before spooning into a serving dish.

Avocado and corn salad (serves 4)

1 medium avocado, peeled, stoned and diced

4oz/100g sweetcorn kernels, blanched

4oz/100g tomato, skinned, chopped and drained

4oz/100g red pepper, finely chopped

1 small red onion, peeled

1 garlic clove, crushed

1 small red chilli, deseeded and finely chopped

1 rounded tablespoon finely chopped fresh coriander

1 dessertspoon lime juice

black pepper

shredded lettuce

Cut a few rings from the onion for garnish. Finely chop the rest of the onion and mix it with the other ingredients apart from the lettuce. Serve on a bed of lettuce, garnished with the onion rings.

Chickpea and pepper salad (serves 4)

8oz/225g cooked chickpeas

4oz/100g red pepper, chopped

4oz/100g yellow pepper, chopped

4oz/100g tomato, skinned and chopped

1 small red onion, peeled and finely chopped

2 garlic cloves, crushed

1 small green chilli, deseeded and finely chopped

1 inch/2.5cm piece of root ginger, finely chopped

1 tablespoon groundnut oil

1 tablespoon finely chopped fresh coriander

1 teaspoon cumin seeds

1 dessertspoon lemon juice

black pepper

Heat the oil and fry the red and yellow peppers, onion, garlic, chilli and ginger until almost soft. Add the cumin seeds and tomato and cook for a further couple of minutes. Remove from the heat and add the chickpeas, coriander and lemon juice. Season with black pepper and mix well. Chill before serving.

SAUCES AND RELISHES

Relishes are commonly served with curries, alongside other little dishes such as chopped banana or sliced cooked plantain sprinkled with lemon or lime juice, freshly grated coconut mixed with finely chopped fresh chillies, bowls of plain yoghurt and plain or spiced peanuts or cashew nuts. They are also ideal for serving with snack foods and like sauces and dressings can be used to liven up plain cooked vegetables and give them an African flavour. Awaze, a traditional Ethiopian dish, can be made hotter if required by adding more chillies.

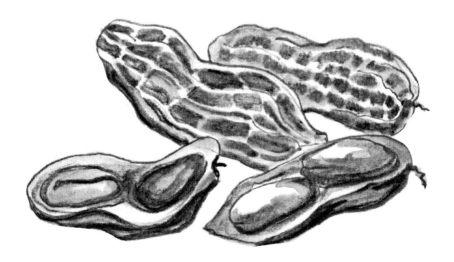

Ethiopian awaze (serves 4)

6oz/175g green peppers, chopped

1 inch/2.5cm piece of root ginger, chopped

1-2 green chillies, finely chopped

1 garlic clove, crushed

1 small onion, peeled and chopped

1 dessertspoon groundnut oil

2 tablespoons finely chopped fresh coriander

1 tablespoon lemon juice

black pepper

Fry the green peppers, ginger, chillies, garlic and onion in the oil until soft. Transfer to a blender and add the coriander and lemon juice. Season with black pepper and blend until fairly smooth. Serve warm or cold as a sauce or dip or add as a flavouring to cooked dishes.

Peanut and coconut sauce (serves 4)

2 rounded tablespoons smooth peanut butter

10 fl.oz/300ml thin coconut milk or 1oz/25g grated creamed
    coconut mixed with 10 fl.oz/300ml warm water

1 small onion, peeled and grated

1 dessertspoon groundnut oil

1 small dried red chilli, crushed

1 dessertspoon cornflour

black pepper

Soften the onion in the oil. Dissolve the cornflour in the coconut milk and add to the pan together with the remaining ingredients. Stir well, then bring to the boil while stirring. Continue stirring for a minute or so until the sauce thickens.

Hot ginger and coriander sauce (serves 4)

1 inch/2.5cm piece of fresh root ginger, grated

1 small onion, peeled and grated

1 small green chilli, deseeded and finely chopped

2 rounded tablespoons finely chopped fresh coriander

1 dessertspoon groundnut oil

10 fl.oz/300ml vegetable stock

1 rounded tablespoon cornflour

black pepper

Heat the oil and fry the ginger, onion and chilli until softened. Mix the cornflour with the vegetable stock until smooth, then add to the pan together with the coriander. Season with black pepper and bring to the boil while stirring. Continue stirring for a minute or two until the sauce thickens.

Banana and yoghurt dressing (serves 4)

8oz/225g ripe bananas, peeled and finely chopped

lemon juice

5 fl.oz/150ml plain soya yoghurt

ground cinnamon

Sprinkle the banana with lemon juice, then mix with the yoghurt. Serve sprinkled with ground cinnamon.

Sudanese chilli and garlic dressing (serves 4)

2 red chillies, very finely chopped

4 garlic cloves, crushed

2 tablespoons lemon juice

1 tablespoon groundnut oil

black pepper

Mix the ingredients until well combined. Use as a dressing for salads or spoon over cooked foods.

Fresh tomato relish (serves 4/6)

12oz/350g ripe tomatoes, skinned and finely chopped

1 small red onion, peeled and finely chopped

1 small red chilli, finely chopped

2 garlic cloves, crushed

1 rounded tablespoon finely chopped fresh coriander

1 tablespoon lemon juice

½ teaspoon paprika

black pepper

Combine the ingredients well.

Mango and ginger relish (serves 4)

8oz/225g firm mango flesh

1 small onion, peeled and finely chopped

1 inch/2.5cm piece of root ginger, finely chopped

1 dessertspoon groundnut oil

1 tablespoon finely chopped fresh coriander

1 tablespoon water

1 tablespoon lemon juice

1 teaspoon brown sugar

¼ teaspoon turmeric

black pepper

Fry the onion and ginger in the oil until soft, then add the remaining ingredients. Stir well and simmer gently, stirring frequently, for about 15 minutes until the mango is soft and the mixture thick. Transfer to a serving bowl, cover and allow to cool before serving.

Sweetcorn relish (serves 4)

8oz/225g sweetcorn kernels

1 medium red onion, peeled and finely chopped

1 red chilli, finely chopped

2 garlic cloves, crushed

1 dessertspoon groundnut oil

½ teaspoon turmeric

1 teaspoon fenugreek seeds

1 teaspoon yellow mustard seeds

4 fl.oz/125ml water

black pepper

Soften the onion in the oil, add the other ingredients and stir well. Bring to the boil, cover and simmer, stirring frequently, for about 10 minutes until the liquid has been absorbed. Remove from the heat and mash before transferring to a serving bowl. Serve warm or cold.

Green tomato and raisin relish (serves 4)

8oz/225g green tomatoes, finely chopped

1 small onion, peeled and finely chopped

1 small green chilli, deseeded and finely chopped

1 garlic clove, crushed

1oz/25g raisins

1oz/25g brown sugar

1 dessertspoon groundnut oil

2 fl.oz/50ml water

¼ teaspoon ground allspice

Fry the onion in the oil until soft, add the remaining ingredients and simmer, stirring frequently, for about 10 minutes until the mixture is thick. Transfer to a serving bowl and chill before serving.

Peach relish (serves 4/6)

12oz/350g ripe peaches, stoned and chopped

1 small red onion, peeled and finely chopped

1oz/25g brown sugar

½oz/15g raisins

1 garlic clove, crushed

1 small red chilli, deseeded and finely chopped

1 dessertspoon groundnut oil

1 tablespoon lemon juice

½ teaspoon ground cloves

½ teaspoon ground ginger

¼ teaspoon turmeric

black pepper

Heat the oil, fry the onion until soft, then add the rest of the ingredients and simmer, stirring frequently, for about 10 minutes until the mixture is thick. Spoon into a bowl and chill before serving.

DESSERTS

Desserts are not always offered at the end of a meal, but if they are they are very likely to consist of fresh locally-grown fruits, which are cheap and abundant in some areas. Delicately flavoured custard-style dishes also feature highly, especially in the Sudan, where crème caramel is a traditional favourite. Rice pudding is a popular dessert in almost every cuisine around the world and in East Africa it is enjoyed flavoured with peanuts. Although they are all suitable for serving as desserts, some of the dishes featured here such as barbecued bananas and fried sweet potato chips are also eaten at other times of the day as snacks.

Fresh fruit salad

Fresh tropical fruits are the preferred choice for dessert in many East African countries. Single fruits are simply served cut into slices, or a mixture of fruits can be cut into chunks and made into a fruit salad. For an authentic tasting East African fruit salad use a selection of fruit from avocado, banana, grapefruit, guava, mango, melon, orange, paw paw, peach, pineapple and passion fruit. Allow 4-5oz/100-150g of prepared fruit, cut into even-sized chunks, per person. Cover with tropical fruit juice and sprinkle with fresh or toasted flaked coconut.

Sudanese crème caramel (serves 4)

16 fl.oz/475ml soya milk
1oz/25g cornflour
1 teaspoon vanilla essence
2oz/50g brown sugar
2 tablespoons water
glacé cherry halves

Put the brown sugar and water in a double boiler and heat while stirring for about 10 minutes, until a spoon drawn through the mixture separates it. Remove the pan from the heat. Mix the cornflour and vanilla essence with the soya milk until smooth, add to the sugar mixture and combine well. Return to the heat and bring to the boil while stirring. Continue stirring for a minute or two until the mixture thickens. Pour it into a serving bowl, cover and chill for a few hours until set, then decorate with glacé cherry halves.

Barbecued bananas (serves 4)

4 large underripe bananas
lemon juice
brown sugar
ground cinnamon

Place the bananas on a hot barbecue or under a hot grill, turning them occasionally, until the skins blacken. Carefully peel them and put them on plates. Sprinkle with lemon juice and a little brown sugar and ground cinnamon and serve.

Mango and yoghurt fool (serves 4)

1lb/450g firm mango flesh, finely chopped

½oz/15g brown sugar

4 tablespoons water

8 fl.oz/225ml plain soya yoghurt

ground cinnamon

Put the mango, sugar and water in a pan and cook, stirring occasionally, for 10 minutes until the mango is soft. Remove from the heat and mash the mango, then spoon it into a bowl, cover and refrigerate until cold. Mix in the yoghurt and divide the fool between 4 glass dishes or bowls. Sprinkle with ground cinnamon.

Fried sweet potato and cinnamon chips (serves 4)

1lb/450g sweet potatoes, peeled

groundnut oil

brown sugar

ground cinnamon

Cut the potatoes into chips and fry in hot oil until golden. Drain on kitchen paper and sprinkle lightly with brown sugar and ground cinnamon.

Tropical fruit and cashew nut crunch (serves 4)

1 paw paw, peeled, deseeded and diced

1 firm banana, peeled and sliced

1 passion fruit

2oz/50g cashew nuts, chopped

1oz/25g plain flour

½oz/15g brown sugar

½oz/15g vegan margarine

⅛ teaspoon ground cloves

Melt the margarine in a small pan, then remove from the heat and add the flour, sugar, cashew nuts and ground cloves and mix thoroughly. Scoop the seeds and pulp from the passion fruit and mix it with the paw paw and banana. Put the fruit in a small baking dish and spoon the cashew nut mixture evenly over the top. Bake in a preheated oven at 180°C/350°F/Gas mark 4 for about 20 minutes until golden brown. Serve hot.

Pineapple and coconut custard cups (serves 4)

1lb/450g pineapple slices in natural juice

12 fl.oz/350ml soya milk

1oz/25g cornflour

1oz/25g creamed coconut, grated

1oz/25g brown sugar

toasted flaked coconut

Strain the pineapple juice into a jug and add the soya milk, cornflour, creamed coconut and sugar. Mix until no lumps remain, then pour into a double boiler and bring to the boil while stirring. Continue stirring for a minute or so until the custard thickens. Chop the pineapple slices and divide them between 4 glass dishes or bowls. Top with the pineapple custard, then keep in the fridge for a few hours until set. Sprinkle toasted flaked coconut on top before serving.

Peanut and rice pudding (serves 4)

4oz/100g long grain rice

2oz/50g peanuts, ground and roasted

10 fl.oz/300ml water

10 fl.oz/300ml soya milk

1oz/25g brown sugar

chopped roasted peanuts

Bring the rice and water to the boil, cover and simmer until the liquid has been absorbed. Remove from the heat and add the ground peanuts, soya milk and sugar. Mix thoroughly and return to a low heat. Simmer, stirring occasionally, for about 10 minutes, until the milk has been absorbed and the mixture has thickened. Spoon into 4 bowls and serve warm, garnished with chopped peanuts.

Paw paw and coconut ice (serves 4)

1 large paw paw, peeled, deseeded and diced

1 tablespoon brown sugar

1 tablespoon water

½oz/15g creamed coconut, grated

9 fl.oz/250ml soya cream

toasted flaked coconut

Put the paw paw, sugar and water in a small pan and cook for about 5 minutes until pulpy. Add the creamed coconut and stir until it dissolves, then remove from the heat and mash smooth. Add the soya cream, mix well and pour the mixture into a shallow freezerproof container. Cover and freeze for 30 minutes, then whisk the mixture with a fork and return to the freezer for a few hours until just solid. If the ice becomes too hard keep it at room temperature for 45 minutes before serving. Scoop into serving dishes and sprinkle with toasted flaked coconut.

Passion fruit and orange mousse (serves 4)

6 passion fruits

8 fl.oz/225ml fresh orange juice

8 fl.oz/225ml soya milk

1oz/25g cornflour

1oz/25g brown sugar

Scoop the pulp and seeds from 4 of the passion fruits into a saucepan, add the orange juice and bring to the boil. Cover and simmer for 2 minutes, then strain the juice into a jug, pressing out as much pulp as possible with the back of a spoon. Mix the cornflour and sugar with the soya milk until smooth, add to the juice and stir until well combined. Pour into a double boiler and bring to the boil while stirring. Continue stirring until the sauce thickens, then pour into 4 individual dishes. Cover and chill until set and garnish with the pulp and seeds from the remaining passion fruits before serving.

CAKES AND PASTRIES

Ingredients such as bananas, peanuts, coconut, cinnamon, cloves and allspice are synonymous with East African cuisine and all of these are put to good use in creating a variety of delicious cakes and pastries.

Sweet potatoes too are ideal for sweet dishes and they are used particularly to make moist and flavourful cakes and flan fillings. East Africans are very fond of fried cakes and some of the examples here are typical of those that can be bought ready-made from street vendors.

Variations of fruit-filled flans are found all over the region, with different fruits being used according to what is available or in season.

Fried banana and peanut cakes (makes 8)

8oz/225g banana, peeled and lightly mashed

2oz/50g rice flour

1oz/25g plain flour

1oz/25g peanuts, finely chopped and roasted

4 fl.oz/125ml soya milk

pinch of ground cinnamon

groundnut oil

lemon juice

brown sugar

Put the rice flour and plain flour in a mixing bowl with the soya milk and cinnamon and combine thoroughly, then mix in the banana and peanuts. Heat a small amount of oil in a non-stick pan until hot and fry rounded table-spoonfuls of the mixture for a few minutes on each side until golden. Drain the cakes on kitchen paper and sprinkle lightly with lemon juice and brown sugar.

Spiced Zanzibar date cake

6oz/175g dried dates, finely chopped

4oz/100g self raising flour

2oz/50g rice flour

1oz/25g brown sugar

2 fl.oz/50ml groundnut oil

4 fl.oz/125ml water

4 fl.oz/125ml fresh apple juice

½ teaspoon ground cloves

½ teaspoon ground cinnamon

Put 4oz/100g of the dates in a small pan with the water and bring to the boil. Cover and simmer for a few minutes until the liquid has been absorbed, then remove from the heat and mash the dates to a thick purée with the back of a spoon. Transfer this to a large bowl and add the rice flour, sugar, oil and spices.

Now add the remaining dates, flour and apple juice and mix thoroughly. Spoon the mixture into a base-lined and greased 7 inch/18cm square baking tin and level the top. Bake in a preheated oven at 180°C/350°F/Gas mark 4 for about 25 minutes until browned and firm. Allow to cool before cutting into slices.

Sweet potato and coconut tart (serves 6)

pastry
4oz/100g self raising flour

1½oz/40g vegan margarine

cold water

filling
8oz/225g sweet potatoes, peeled and diced

3oz/75g self raising flour

1oz/25g creamed coconut, grated

1oz/25g brown sugar

½oz/15g vegan margarine

¼ teaspoon ground allspice

3 fl.oz/75ml soya milk

desiccated coconut

Make the pastry by rubbing the margarine into the flour and adding enough water to bind. Knead the dough well and turn out onto a floured board. Roll out to line a greased loose-bottomed shallow 8 inch/20cm diameter flan tin. Prick the base all over with a fork and bake blind in a preheated oven at 180°C/350°F/Gas mark 4 for 5 minutes.

Boil the potatoes, drain, dry off over a low heat and mash them. Put the creamed coconut, sugar and margarine in a saucepan and heat gently until melted. Remove from the heat and stir in the mashed potato. Add the flour, ground allspice and soya milk and combine thoroughly. Spoon the mixture evenly into the pastry flan case and sprinkle the top with desiccated coconut. Return to the oven and bake for 20-25 minutes until golden brown. Allow to cool slightly in the tin before cutting into wedges and serving warm.

Vitambua (makes 12)

6oz/175g rice flour

6oz/175g plain flour

1oz/25g brown sugar

1 rounded teaspoon easy-blend yeast

8 cardamom pods, husked

8 fl.oz/225ml thin coconut milk, warmed

groundnut oil for frying

Mix the two flours with the sugar and yeast. Crush the cardamom seeds and add to the bowl together with the coconut milk. Combine well, then cover the bowl and leave in a warm place for 1 hour.

Shallow fry rounded tablespoonfuls of the mixture, flattening them out with the back of a spoon, in hot oil for a few minutes on each side until golden. Drain on kitchen paper and serve warm.

Peanut and millet biscuits (makes 8)

2oz/50g millet flour

2oz/50g self raising flour

1oz/25g brown sugar

1 rounded tablespoon peanut butter

1 tablespoon groundnut oil

cold water

Mix the sugar with the peanut butter and oil in a large bowl. Add the two flours and stir until crumbly, then gradually add enough cold water to make a soft dough. Take rounded dessertspoonfuls of the mixture and roll into balls. Flatten these into biscuits and put them on a greased baking sheet. Indent the tops with a fork and bake in a preheated oven at 180°C/350°F/Gas mark 4 for about 15 minutes until browned. Allow to cool before serving.

Banana and coconut cake

6oz/175g ripe bananas, peeled and mashed

4oz/100g self raising flour

2oz/50g rice flour

2oz/50g vegan margarine

1½oz/40g brown sugar

½ teaspoon ground allspice

½ teaspoon vanilla essence

4 fl.oz/125ml thin coconut milk

desiccated coconut

Mix the self raising flour with the rice flour and allspice, rub in the margarine, then stir in the sugar and vanilla essence. Add the mashed banana and coconut milk and combine thoroughly. Spoon the mixture into a base-lined and greased 6 inch/15cm round baking tin and level the top. Sprinkle with desiccated coconut and bake in a preheated oven at 180°C/350°F/Gas mark 4 for about 25 minutes until golden. Leave to cool on a wire rack.

Tropical fruit flan (serves 6)

pastry
6oz/175g self raising flour

2½oz/65g vegan margarine

cold water

filling
12oz/350g mango flesh, chopped

½oz/15g brown sugar

6 cloves

2 fl.oz/50ml soya milk

¼oz/7g cornflour

8oz/225g bananas, peeled and sliced

lemon juice

2 passion fruits

toasted flaked coconut

Rub the margarine into the flour and add enough water to bind. Knead the dough well, then turn it out onto a floured board and roll it out to line a greased loose-bottomed deep 8inch/20cm flan tin. Prick the base all over with a fork and bake blind in a preheated oven at 180°C/350°F/Gas mark 4 for 15-20 minutes until golden brown. Allow to cool in the tin while making the filling.

Put the mango, sugar and cloves in a saucepan and cook gently until pulpy. Remove from the heat, discard the cloves and mash the fruit smooth. Mix the cornflour with the soya milk and add to the fruit. Mix well, return the pan to the stove and heat gently while stirring until the mixture thickens. Allow to cool slightly, then spoon the mixture evenly into the cooled flan case. Cover and refrigerate until cold.

Sprinkle the banana slices with lemon juice and arrange them on top of the mango purée. Scoop out the flesh and seeds from the passion fruits and spoon over the banana slices. Garnish with a little flaked coconut.

Sweet potato and peanut cake

8oz/225g sweet potatoes, peeled and diced

4oz/100g self raising flour

2oz/50g peanuts, ground and roasted

2oz/50g raisins

1½oz/40g brown sugar

2 tablespoons groundnut oil

½ teaspoon ground allspice

5 fl.oz/150ml soya milk

chopped peanuts

Cook the sweet potatoes, drain and mash. Mix the flour with the ground peanuts, sugar and allspice in a large bowl. Stir in the oil, then rub it in with the fingertips until well combined. Stir in the raisins and mashed potato, add the soya milk and mix thoroughly. Spoon the mixture into a base-lined and greased 7 inch/18cm round baking tin and level the top. Sprinkle with chopped peanuts and press these in lightly with the back of a spoon. Bake in a preheated oven at 180°C/350°F/Gas mark 4 for 30-35 minutes until browned. Transfer to a wire rack to cool.

Banana maandazi (makes 8)

8oz/225g plain flour

4oz/100g ripe banana, peeled and mashed

1oz/25g brown sugar

1 teaspoon easy-blend yeast

½ teaspoon ground cinnamon

1 tablespoon groundnut oil

approx. 2½ fl.oz/65ml warm water

extra oil

Mix the flour with the sugar, yeast and cinnamon. Stir in the tablespoonful of oil, then add the banana and combine thoroughly. Gradually add enough water to make a soft dough. Turn this out onto a floured board and knead well. Return the dough to the bowl, cover and leave in a warm place for 1 hour. Knead the dough again on a floured board and divide it into 8 equal pieces. Roll each one into a ball, flatten them slightly and put them on a tray. Leave in a warm place for 30 minutes, then shallow fry in hot oil for a few minutes on each side until golden. Drain on kitchen paper.

DRINKS

Freshly squeezed orange and grapefruit juice are widely drunk in areas where citrus fruits are grown and other locally-grown tropical fruits are blended to make delicious refreshing drinks. These are made at home or bought ready-made from drinks stalls in the market place. The stalls also sell a wide variety of fruit juice concentrates, which are diluted with water and served with meals.

European settlers established the first tea and coffee plantations in wetter areas of the region and nowadays plantations have been expanded and tea and coffee exports are a major source of income, especially in Kenya, Tanzania and Ethiopia. Both tea and coffee are enjoyed throughout the day and they are served in various ways in different countries. In the Sudan coffee beans are roasted over charcoal and then ground with cloves, to give a very distinctive flavour. Coffee flavoured with ginger is a favourite drink in Eritrea and all over the region tea is flavoured with cinnamon or cardamom and drunk either with or without milk and often sweetened with large amounts of sugar.

Pomegranate and orange juice (serves 4)

2 large pomegranates

1 tablespoon brown sugar

16 fl.oz/475ml water

10 fl.oz/300ml chilled fresh orange juice

crushed ice

4 slices of orange

Scoop the pomegranate seeds into a saucepan and add the water and sugar. Bring to the boil, cover and simmer for 5 minutes, then refrigerate until cold. Strain the juice into a jug, pressing out as much as possible with the back of a spoon. Add the orange juice and mix well. Pour into glasses, add crushed ice and garnish each glass with a slice of orange.

Peach fruit cocktail (serves 4)

8oz/225g peaches, stoned and chopped

2 passion fruits

8 fl.oz/225ml chilled fresh orange juice

8 fl.oz/225ml chilled fresh pineapple juice

¼oz/7g brown sugar

2 tablespoons water

crushed ice

Scoop the passion fruit flesh and pips into a fine sieve over a small saucepan. Press out the flesh and juice with the back of a spoon, leaving only the pips in the sieve. Add the peaches, water and sugar to the pan and cook for a few minutes until soft. Chill the fruit, then blend smooth with the orange and pineapple juice. Pour into glasses and add crushed ice.

Melon and coconut cocktail (serves 4)

8oz/225g peeled orange-fleshed melon, chopped

8 fl.oz/225ml coconut milk

10 fl.oz/300ml chilled water

melon balls

Blend the chopped melon with the coconut milk and water until smooth. Pour into glasses and add melon balls.

Mango and apple squash (serves 4)

8oz/225g firm mango flesh, chopped

8 fl.oz/225ml water

½oz/15g brown sugar

16 fl.oz/475ml fresh apple juice

crushed ice

Put the mango, water and sugar in a pan and bring to the boil. Cover and simmer for 5 minutes, then pour into a blender and blend smooth. Put in the fridge until cold, then mix in the apple juice. Strain through a fine sieve, stir well, pour into glasses and add crushed ice.

Paw paw and pineapple shake (serves 4)

6oz/175g ripe paw paw flesh, chopped

10 fl.oz/300ml chilled pineapple juice

8 fl.oz/225ml chilled soya milk

1 tablespoon brown sugar

crushed ice

Blend the paw paw with the pineapple juice, soya milk and sugar until smooth. Add crushed ice when serving.

Peanut and banana shake (serves 4)

2 rounded tablespoons smooth peanut butter

8oz/225g ripe bananas, peeled and chopped

24 fl.oz/725ml soya milk

ground cinnamon

Blend the peanut butter with the bananas and soya milk until smooth, then pour into glasses and sprinkle with ground cinnamon.

Passion fruit and pineapple juice (serves 4)

4 passion fruits

16 fl.oz/475ml water

1 tablespoon brown sugar

12 fl.oz/350ml chilled fresh pineapple juice

crushed ice

pineapple cubes

Scoop the passion fruit seeds and pulp into a saucepan and add the water and sugar. Bring to the boil, cover and simmer for 5 minutes, then refrigerate until cold. Strain the liquid into a jug, pressing out as much pulp as possible with the back of a spoon, and mix in the pineapple juice. Add crushed ice and pineapple cubes to each glass when serving.